Public Administration and the State

Public Administration and the State

A Postmodern Perspective

Michael W. Spicer

THE UNIVERSITY OF ALABAMA PRESS
TUSCALOOSA

Designer: Paul Moxon
Typeface: Janson

The paper on which this book is printed meets the minimum
requirements of American National Standard for Information
Science–Permanence of Paper for Printed Library Materials,
ANSI Z39.48–1984.

Library of Congress Cataloging-in-Publication Data

Spicer, Michael W.
  Public administration and the state : a postmodern perspective /
Michael W. Spicer.
      p. cm.
Includes bibliographical references and index.
   ISBN 0-8173-52392 (pbk. : alk. paper)
1. Public administration. 2. Political science—Philosophy. 3. State,
The. I. Title.
  JF1351 .S585 2001
  351'.01—dc21   2001001823

British Library Cataloguing-in-Publication Data available

To Claudia

Contents

Preface   ix

1
The Neglect of the State   1

2
The Vision of a Purposive State   13

3
The Prussian Experience and the Purposive State   33

4
American Public Administration and the Purposive State   51

5
The Practical Limits of Teleocracy   70

6
Postmodernity and the State   89

7
Public Administration in a Civil Association   109

8
Implications for Public Administration Enquiry   125

References   141

Index   153

Preface

This book is about public administration and our ideas about what constitutes a state. Consistent with my past writing, it is an attempt to show how political philosophy and history can be made relevant to the study and practice of contemporary public administration. I argue here specifically that much of our literature in public administration, despite its frequent claims to political and ideological neutrality, advances a very strong and politically value-laden vision of the state as a collective enterprise driven by some set of substantive ends or purposes. I explore the philosophical and historical roots of this vision of the state and also the problems that it creates for public administration discourse in light of our constitutional and political traditions and our currently fragmented postmodern political culture. Furthermore, I examine an alternative vision of the state as a civil association, one in which individuals, groups, and organizations are seen as free to pursue a variety of interests and ends within a framework of a set of rules of conduct. This vision, I argue, is not only more consistent with our traditions of political and administrative practice but also may be more useful to us in navigating the postmodern political condition in which we find ourselves.

What distinguishes this book from many others in our field is that it attempts to relate a rather broad range of philosophical ideas, both modern and postmodern, to public administration thinking and practice while, at the same time, paying attention to some of the neglected, but important detailed passages of European and American administrative history. I hope that, as a result, the book will prove both informative and enjoyable to readers, whether or not they agree with all of its arguments, and, furthermore, that it may even stimulate some of them to draw more upon philosophy and history, as they think about, write about, teach, study, and even practice public administration.

I would like to thank various publishers for permission to reprint in this book portions of the following articles written by me. Most of these are divided up among several chapters of the book, and all have been extensively revised: (1) "The Science of Administration, the Founders, and Theories of Political Association," *International Journal of Public Administration* 21, nos. 2–4 (1998):299–321, copyright ©1998 by Marcel Dekker, Inc., reprinted from above by courtesy of Marcel Dekker, Inc.; (2) "Public Administration, the State, and the Postmodern Condition," *American Behavioral Scientist* 41, no. 1 (1997):90–102, copyright ©1997 by Sage Publications, reprinted by permission of Sage Publications, Inc.; (3) "Public Administration, Social Science, and Political Association," *Administration and Society* 30, no. 1 (1998):35–52, copyright ©1998 by Sage Publications, reprinted by permission of Sage Publications, Inc.; (4) "Frederick the Great on Government and Public Administration: An Examination of His Ideas and Their Significance for American Public Administration," *American Review of Public Administration* 28, no. 3 (1998):287–305, copyright ©1998 by Sage Publications, reprinted by permission of Sage Publications, Inc.; (5) "Cameralist Thought and Public Administration," *Journal of Management History* 4, no. 3 (1998):149–159, copyright ©1998 by MCB University Press; and (6) "Public Administration under 'Enlightened Despotism' in Prussia: An Examination of Frederick the Great's Administrative Practice," *Administrative Theory and Praxis* 20, no. 1 (1998):23–31, copyright ©1998 by the Public Administration Theory Network. Also, chapter 7 draws in part from my article "Justices of the Peace in Stuart England," *Public Voices* 4, no. 3 (2000):7–27.

I would like to thank my colleagues at Cleveland State University and also with the Public Administration Theory Network, conversations with whom did much to help the progress of this book. Thanks are also due to Cleveland State University for providing me with the academic leave and other resources necessary to complete this project. Finally, special thanks are due to my wife, Claudia, who, drawing on her skills as a librarian, helped me prepare the index for this book.

. . . .

I

The Neglect of the State

This book is about American public administration and the idea of
the state. That the idea of the state should have some relevance to
public administration might seem obvious to any ordinary reader; indeed, such relevance is assumed in much of the European writings on
public administration. With a few notable exceptions (Waldo 1984;
Rohr 1986; Stillman 1991; Skowronek 1982), however, American writers
on public administration have typically devoted little explicit attention
to the idea of the state. As Richard Stillman has observed, "Not many
American scholars until recently have attempted to study the *state*, or
even dare mention *state* in a book title" (1997, 332). Fundamental ideas
about the character of a state, such as "Why should we obey government laws?" "What is the relationship between citizens and government?" or "What ought to be the nature of the engagements, activities,
and responsibilities of our government?" are rarely addressed explicitly in our literature. This neglect of the state is especially evident among
our more contemporary writers. The question as to what constitutes a
good public administration has frequently been seen as one that can be
examined separately from any particular vision of a state. Of course,
the practical politics of administration, including the interactions between public administrators and elected officials, interest groups, and
citizens, has certainly been examined at some length. Nevertheless,
political theory as such has generally been ignored. Many public administration writers seem to continue to hold to the view, expressed
some sixty years ago by Lyndall Urwick, that human organizations can
be examined without regard to "any constitutional, political or social
theory underlying [their] creation" (1937, 49).

Why Do We Neglect the State?
Why is it that so many writers in American public administration
have neglected the idea of the state? Such neglect may perhaps reflect
a certain uneasiness, a certain lack of comfort on the part of public
administration writers with the idea of the state. In this regard, it is

probably true to say that Americans in general are rather wary of the idea of the state. They are more ambivalent than are Europeans about the kind of governmental power over the lives of citizens that such an entity would seem to entail. Stillman has observed here that Americans have always had a preference for what he calls "statelessness." He notes that Americans believe "that the nation ideally should get along without state machinery designed to make government function" (1990, 166). According to Stillman, they generally "feel it is best to let things work out 'naturally' without the constraints or demands of an artificially imposed state" (166). This has been reflected in the development of our administrative system, which, as Stillman observes, "grew piecemeal, attempting to cope with the shocks of change in an ad hoc manner and without any one grand design" (1991, 68). In light of this strong vein of antistatism in our culture, it is to be expected perhaps then that American public administration writers would not devote very much time or attention to the idea of the state.

A further reason for the neglect of the state by American public administration writers may be their strongly pragmatic bent. Public administration, as a field of enquiry, after all, has always had a practical or a problem-focused orientation toward its subject matter. Indeed, public administration writers have frequently involved themselves in the practice of public administration whether as practitioners, at some phase in their careers, or as consultants or as activists. It may be, therefore, that many public administration writers simply believe that the exploration of the seemingly esoteric political philosophy and theory, which surrounds the question of the nature of the state, is of little practical value to them as they think and go about making concrete recommendations about administrative practice. Indeed, Dwight Waldo has noted that pragmatism, interpreted not as a formal philosophy but rather "broadly as a mood, a temper, an approach, continues importantly as a part of public administration" (1984, xxxviii). Waldo suggests that public administration writers are inclined to share the pragmatic belief of their fellow Americans that practical considerations, such as "what will work best—or at least work?" are "likely to be more crucial than either abstract philosophy on the one hand or administrative principles or economic formulae on the other" (1984, xxxviii).

Moreover, whereas pragmatism may have caused some public administration writers to ignore the state, the desire among other writers to render public administration more scientific may also have contributed to its neglect. More than a few public administration writers, following the lead of such positivists as Herbert Simon, have sought to focus the attention of the field of public administration on relatively narrow and well-defined empirical questions, which seem readily amenable to scientific investigation, rather than on broad and enduring questions of political philosophy, which are difficult or even impossible to reduce to empirically testable hypotheses. Such writers have tended to accept Simon's edict that, if public administration is to be a science, it must be "concerned purely with factual statements" and that "there is no basis for ethical assertions in the body of a science" (1976, 253). To writers of such a positivist bent, the question of what should be the character of a state is one that is simply far too heavily laden with questions of ethics or values to enable meaningful enquiry. Such a question is, from a scientific perspective, therefore, irrelevant. Writers such as Simon argue that what is needed rather "is empirical research and experimentation to determine the relative desirability of alternative administrative arrangements" (1976, 42). Simon himself asserts the irrelevance of questions about the character of the state to administrative science when he argues that "the process of valuation [of ends] lies outside the scope of science" and that "efficiency, whether it be in the democratic state or the totalitarian, is the proper criterion to be applied to the factual element in the decision problem" (184).

Finally, public administration's neglect of the state almost certainly has intellectual roots in the enduring idea, advanced by early writers such as Woodrow Wilson (1887), that it is possible somehow to separate the administrative activities of governance from the activities of politics: the so-called politics-administration dichotomy. Although frequently buried by critics such as Waldo (1984), this idea, which was arguably central to the establishment of the field of public administration, continues to come back and haunt us. Waldo himself has referred here to the "perdurability of the politics-administration dichotomy" (1983, 219), and David Rosenbloom has argued that it "continues to define a good deal of administrative thought" (1993, 503). Self-styled reinventors of government, for example, call for a separation of "policy decisions (steering) from service delivery (rowing)" (Osborne and Gaebler 1993, 35), a distinction that clearly parallels the dichotomy.

Why has the politics-administration dichotomy fostered the neglect of the idea of the state by public administration? It is because it has encouraged the idea that the administrative activities of government can somehow be examined in isolation from questions of politics. Acceptance of the dichotomy appears to render political, as well as constitutional, questions unimportant to the study of public administration. It appears to free administrative scholars from the need to worry about the character of the state. In other words, the effect of the dichotomy is to deflect our attention away from politics and, thereby, away from questions about the character of the state.

Possible reasons for the neglect of the idea of the state by American public administration writers include, therefore, an uneasiness among writers with the idea of the state itself, the strongly pragmatic bent of many public administration writers, the aspirations of many writers to make the study of public administration more scientific, and the politics-administration dichotomy. Whatever the reasons for the neglect of the state, however, a certain paradox exists here. Although public administration writers have not typically troubled themselves very much with exploring and discussing questions of political and constitutional theory, as this book will argue, a very strong and politically value-laden vision of the state can be discerned in the language of much of their writings. In order to provide some preliminary indication of this vision, it may be useful to look more closely at the writings of the reinventing government movement.

The Vision of the State in the Reinventing Government Movement

During the past eight years or so, the reinventing government movement has emerged as almost a new orthodoxy within public administration both in the United States and across the developed world. The central doctrines of this new orthodoxy include eliminating what is seen as burdensome red tape, holding administrators accountable for measurable results, emphasizing customer satisfaction in agency dealings with the public, empowering employees on the front line to make their own decisions, contracting out with the private sector for public service delivery, and securing better value for our tax dollars. Much is made here of the idea that the problems of government are managerial rather than political and that the solution to these problems is administrative reform rather than new public policies or, for that matter, new political institutions. Reinventing government is, according to its advocates, politically and ideologically neutral. Its focus is primarily on "*how* government should work, not on *what* it should do" (Gore 1993, ii). Its principles are applicable "regardless of party, regardless of ideology" (6). Furthermore, these principles can be applied universally across all kinds of political systems with quite different political ideologies and traditions. According to reinventors, their strategies "work in small cities and large nations, in parliamentary systems and presidential systems, in strong mayor cities and council-manager cities" (Osborne and Plastrik 1997, 44). Different types of political systems and organizations may require different tactics, in their view, but "none of these differences changes the basic levers that create fundamental change" so that "reinvention applies to all types of organizations" (Osborne and Plastrik 1997, 47).

All this suggests, at first glance, that the reinventors are trying conscientiously to avoid advancing any particular theory or vision of the state at all. On closer examination of their writings, however, there emerges a rather definite vision of the type of state that they would like to see. Key to understanding this vision, in my view, is their central argument that the activities of government can and should be organized and directed around some coherent set of clearly defined substantive ends or missions. In other words, the activities of government are viewed in almost exclusively teleocratic terms. David Osborne and Ted Gaebler, for example, make explicit their teleocratic vision of governance when they assert that we need to move from "rule-driven government . . . locked up by rules and line-items" to what they term "mission-driven government" with "mission-driven organizations . . . that turn their employees free to pursue the organization's mission with the most effective methods they can find" (1993, 112–113). In their view this change requires, among other things, "hashing out the fundamental purpose of an organization, . . . agreeing on one basic mission," and "organizing by mission rather than by turf" (130–132).

Echoing Osborne and Gaebler, former vice president Al Gore's National Performance Review report (NPR) argues that "effective, entrepreneurial governments cast aside red tape" and "streamline their budget, personnel, and procurement systems—liberating organizations to pursue their missions" (Gore 1993, 6). The reinventing of government requires that we "create a clear sense of mission" and that we "steer more, row less" (7). "Boats travel much faster," says the NPR, "when everyone is pulling their oar in the same direction" (Gore 1993, 75). The president is urged here to follow the example of the handling of the Allied Expeditionary Force in World War II, where General Eisenhower "was given a mission statement that clearly delineated goals"; also cited is the example of President Kennedy, who "gave NASA an even clearer mission: Put a man on the moon and return him safely to earth by the end of the decade" (75).

Consistent with their vision of purpose-driven or teleocratic governance, reinventors believe that government should seek to emulate the practices of other teleocratic organizations, most especially those of business organizations. In this regard, the NPR, noting that "through the ages, public management has tended to follow the prevailing paradigm of private management," is clearly impressed by how "major American corporations have revolutionized the way they do business" (Gore 1993, 8). In order to reinvent government, says the NPR, "we must seek the guidance of those who have successfully transformed large organizations in both the private and public sectors" (121). Although conceding that differences exist between the public and private sector, these reinventors argue, nonetheless, that "we *can* transplant some aspects of the business world into the public arena. We can create an environment that commits federal managers to the same struggle to cut costs and improve customer service that compels private managers. We can imbue the federal government—from top to bottom—with a driving sense of accountability" (Gore 1993, 43).

One might think here that these reinventors just want to improve administrative practices. Their recommendations, however, suggest something significantly more ambitious. Congress, for example, is specifically scolded in the NPR report for giving agencies "multiple missions, some of which are contradictory" (Gore 1993, 13), and it is urged to "clarify the objectives of federal programs" (74). Congress is also urged to eliminate policies and programs "that serve special, not national interests" (94). Furthermore, in discussing reforms in the budgetary process, the NPR report asserts that the budget should reflect what it terms "the thoughtful planning of our public leaders" and should not simply be "the product of struggles among competing interests" (15). In other words, the reinventors want government as a whole, not just public administrators, to behave in a more rational and teleocratic fashion. Indeed, Richard Nathan not only recognizes but also clearly welcomes the teleocratic model of governance that appears to undergird the reinventing movement. Nathan sees within this movement the real possibility of "toning down" what he calls "the hyperpluralism of American government" so that "hard problems can be addressed more easily and more expeditiously," so that we can "get policy closure on high-salience issues," and so that we can "bring competence to bear in the implementation of these new policies once adopted" (1995, 215).

Finally, we should observe here that the reinventors themselves are fairly open about their vision of teleocratic governance. Osborne and Gaebler, for example, boldly call for what they term "an entrepreneurial revolution" based on "the shared vision and goals of a community" (1993, 327). They urge "entrepreneurial leaders" to "rally their communities to their visions" and to gain support from "enough of the community" so as "to overcome the opposition" to "the leaders' vision" (327). Also, in reviewing progress on federal reinventing government efforts, the NPR makes evident its vision of teleocratic governance when it argues that "common sense government . . . means a government that focuses on results" and that "moves heaven and earth to make it easy for citizens, businesses, and state and local governments to meet the nation's common goals" (Gore 1995, 38). Evidently, then, the efforts of not only federal administrators and elected officials but also the entire national community are to be harnessed in support of the pursuit of national purposes or ends.

Despite the claims of the reinventors to political and ideological neutrality, an examination of their rhetoric reveals, therefore, that they express a rather definite vision of the state. What is intimated in their writings is a vision of the state as an association of citizens organized and led by an energetic government in the pursuit of some clearly defined set of substantive missions or ends. Within this vision, the activity of governance becomes akin to that of a business enterprise. As James Carroll argues, it is a vision of "government as a Walmart" (1995, 310). Interestingly enough, this is hardly a new vision of the state. It is, in fact, one that was articulated eloquently by Sir Francis Bacon nearly four centuries ago and one that has its roots in the very emergence of the modern state itself. It is a vision of the state as what I shall term in this book a "purposive association" or a "purposive" state.

Outlining the Argument

This book will argue that the reinventors are by no means alone among public administration writers in advancing a political vision of a powerful purposive state. It will examine and critique this vision of the state that seems to undergird so much of academic thinking about public administration. As such, this book builds on the work of Waldo (1984) and others who have sought to explore and reveal the political theories that underlie the often seemingly politically neutral language of much of American public administration thought. We shall begin here in chapter 2 with an exploration of the character of this vision of a purposive state, as well as its philosophical and historical roots, drawing in large part on the thinking of the late Michael Oakeshott, an English political theorist and philosopher. Special attention will be directed toward the role of the development of an apparatus of administration by European autocratic monarchs and its importance in helping to sustain the idea of a state as a purposive association.

Following this discussion, in chapter 3 I will examine the political and administrative experience of eighteenth-century Prussia under Frederick the Great and the cameralists as an example of a purposive state, both in action and in thought. Such a focus is justified, in my view, for at least two reasons. First, our ideas about the state do not emerge in a vacuum, but rather reflect an attempt to abstract from the concrete social practices of human beings either in government or, for that matter, elsewhere. As will be shown in this book, although the Prussians by no means invented the vision of a purposive state, the example of the Prussian experience in politics and administration under Frederick played a not insignificant role in nourishing, inspiring, and shaping this vision. Second, as I shall also argue, the Prussian example may have had at least some influence on the early development of American public administration as a field of enquiry, although, as will be noted, obviously other influences were also important.

Chapter 4 will be devoted to an exploration of the ways in which the vision of a purposive state has been expressed in the literature of American public administration. Particular attention will be paid here to the vision of governance and administration expressed in the public administration orthodoxy of such writers as Woodrow Wilson, Frederick Taylor, and Luther Gulick, as well as their critics. Attention will also be directed to the vision of the state expressed in a wide variety of contemporary writings in policy analysis and public administration, including those of Herbert Simon.

Chapter 5 will provide the beginnings of a critical view of this idea of a purposive state. The chapter will examine the practical problems that this vision of the state creates for American public policy formulation and administration. I shall explore here the conflict between a purposive state and the vision of the state as a civil association, which is implicit in our constitutional traditions and practices. I will argue that these traditions and practices make it difficult for political leaders to exercise the type of power over administration required to run a purposive state. Furthermore, because these traditions and practices permit relative freedom of action to individuals and groups in society, neither political leaders nor public administrators are likely to possess the knowledge necessary to run a purposive state.

In chapter 6, I shall examine the vision of a purposive state in light of the seriously fragmented character of our postmodern political culture. I will argue that the pursuit of this vision by government can become particularly repressive when different groups of citizens disagree sharply about human ends and values. In chapter 7, I shall draw on the history of the Stuart justices of the peace in England in order to explore an alternative vision of public administration, one that not only is rooted in our constitutional traditions but also is more appropriate to our contemporary political culture. Finally, in chapter 8, following a discussion of the adequacy of our traditions of civil association to the task of modern governance, I will explore directions for future public administration enquiry.

My goal in this book is to help direct the attention of writers, students, and practitioners of public administration and public policy, and perhaps even interested citizens, to the importance of political theory in public administration and, more specifically, to the question of the character of the state and its implications for public administration. In doing so, I seek to provoke a conversation within and, I hope, beyond academia about how we think, write, teach, talk about, and practice public administration. Such a conversation, in my view, has too long been inhibited by the tendency of many administrative scholars and experts to dwell on questions of administrative technique and style. Nevertheless, it is an essential part of the broader ongoing conversation that we have had and should continue to have about the nature of the political community in which we live and the role of a limited constitutional government within it. Furthermore, my hope frankly is that this analysis can help, if only slightly, loosen the grip that the vision of a purposive state has traditionally held over the discipline of public administration and persuade more public administration scholars, educators, and practitioners of the continuing value of a vision of the state that is intimated in our political and constitutional traditions.

The Importance of Visions of the State

Some readers may question the relevance of this type of rather abstract and sometimes normative political theorizing about the state to current public administration thought and practice. I have mentioned already, after all, how the pragmatic character of the field, as well as its aspirations to be more scientific, both work against an exploration and discussion of the idea of a state. This tendency to shy away from abstract normative political theory is not unique to public administration, and, in fact, it pervades a great deal of contemporary social science. It can be discerned even among "return to the state" writers within political science and sociology, who urge a renewed focus on the state in examining political and social processes. These writers advise us that "little is to be gained from more grand theorizing about the state" (Evans, Rueschemeyer, and Skocpol 1985, 363). They recommend instead that we develop a "better understanding of the roots and consequences of state actions and capacities . . . free of automatic activations of visions of what states ought to do or ought not to do" (364).

I would argue that it is difficult, if not impossible, however, to think, speak, or write about public administration in the absence of some sort of broad conceptual vision of governance and the state, whether that vision is explicit or implicit, comprehensive or piecemeal. No matter how carefully we try and separate our political and ethical ideas from our views on public administration, the task is close to impossible. So much of the vocabulary that we use in public administration can acquire meaning only in the context of the particular mental frameworks or categories of thought that we use in thinking about and making sense of government actions. The meanings of such words as *public administration, government, constitution, law, democracy, citizen,* and *legislature* are inherently ambiguous and never precise or neutral in any scientific sense. They are inevitably tied, in the final analysis, to what sort of institution we think government is, can be, or ought to be. They are inextricably linked through our mental frameworks to what it is that we think government does, can do, or ought to do. As the late Isaiah Berlin argued, it is "nearly impossible" to "achieve neutrality" in statements about "moral and social life" because "the words themselves are inescapably charged with ethical or aesthetic or political content" (1979, 157). As a result, no matter how neutral we try to be, whenever we think about human action in a governmental setting, such thinking is likely to reflect some sort of vision of both ethics and politics. As Berlin observed with respect to the empirical study of government,

> Those who confine themselves to observation of human behavior and empirical hypotheses about it . . . tend to analyse men's social and political ideas in the light of some overriding belief of their own—for example, that the purpose of all life is or should be the service of God, however interpreted; or on the contrary that it is the pursuit of experimentally discovered individual or collective satisfaction; or that it lies in the self-realization of a historical (or psychological or aesthetic) pattern, grasp of which alone can explain men to themselves and give meaning to their thoughts and actions; or, on the contrary, that there exists no human purpose; or that men cannot but seek conflicting ends; or cannot (without ceasing to be human) avoid activities that must end in self-frustration, so that the very notion of a final solution is an absurdity" (1979, 167).

In other words, moral and political values permeate the categories or presuppositions that we bring to the examination of the facts of human experience and action in government. They shape the very language we use to describe them. In light of this, therefore, the reader should not be surprised at my argument that public administration writers, although often professing political neutrality, advance, if sometimes only implicitly, quite powerful and value-laden visions of the state and governance. The problem here is not that, in thinking about public administration, we express particular political visions. We cannot help but do so, and we are entitled to do so. The problem is rather that, in our desire either to be more practical or to meet the canons of a more precise value-free social science, we often express those visions unconsciously or without thinking. As a result, we may be led to embrace political values that are incoherent with, or that even contradict, those that we ourselves hold to be dear and true. In Berlin's words, "To neglect the field of political thought" is "merely to allow oneself to remain at the mercy of primitive and uncriticized political beliefs" (1969, 119).

The Vision of a Purposive State

The basic premise of this book is that, despite its frequent attempts to disavow politics, a considerable part of public administration as a field of enquiry has been shaped by a particular vision of politics and the state. In this chapter, I will describe this vision of the state, including the character of its ends and its government, by drawing on the work of Michael Oakeshott and others. I shall then try and show how this vision has been connected to administrative practice across the past three or more centuries. In doing so, my hope is to demonstrate how administrative practice has been deeply implicated in the development of the vision of a purposive state.

The term *state* is, of course, an ambiguous one. Kenneth Dyson has observed that "the evasiveness and ambiguity surrounding state would suggest the impossibility of finding an agreed specific meaning of the term" (1980, 2). To some the state means a particular piece of territory. Others would define it as a collection of particular persons. Still others would equate it with the machinery or the apparatus of government; this is perhaps the most modern view. Richard Stillman, for example, suggests such a view when he defines a state as "concrete national institutions and the organizations and people that carry out the basic functions common to all modern nations" (1991, 15). Theda Skocpol, one of the leading writers in the "return to the state" movement, focusing similarly on the apparatus of government, defines states as "organizations claiming control over territories and people" (1985, 9). Nonetheless, although we should not deny the importance of a governmental apparatus to an understanding of the state, we should also recognize the state as an idea or, as Dyson puts it, a "category of mind" (1980, 3). After all, an organized crime syndicate or cartel might well meet the requirements of Skocpol's definition for a state, but it would not itself, at least for most of us, constitute an idea of a state as such. Also, as Dyson points out, "if anarchy broke out tomorrow, there would be no state apparatus, but the idea of the state would still be present" (1980, 3).

In line with this view of the state as an idea, as opposed to just an apparatus, a state will be seen here, following Oakeshott (1975, 1991, 1993), as representing the terms under which individuals understand their actions to be related to each other and to the actions of their government, that is, the terms of engagement by which individuals see themselves as joined with each other and with their government in a political association. Following from this, a vision of the state can be thought of as simply a narrative or a story that we are used to telling each other and ourselves about the terms of our engagement. Such a narrative is concerned with the activities of governing and being governed. It provides us with an understanding of what it is that we expect our government to be and to do and, for that matter, what we expect our government not to be and not to do. A vision of the state thus also provides us with an understanding of what we feel should be our obligations or duties toward government and toward each other, that is, what we expect of ourselves and others as members of a political association.

The Character of Purposive Association

One of the most powerful visions of the state to shape Western political thought, discourse, and action since the Middle Ages is that of the state as what Oakeshott (1975, 1991) has termed a purposive association, an enterprise association, or, borrowing from Roman law, a *universitas*. A purposive association is a type of political association in which individuals recognize themselves as united or bound together for the joint pursuit of some coherent set of substantive purposes or ends. Individuals within such a state acknowledge themselves and their actions as instrumental to the attainment of the purposes of the state. To use Oakeshott's words, a purposive association is one in which its members see themselves as "related in the joint pursuit of some imagined and wished-for common satisfaction" (1975, 114), "as engaged upon the joint enterprise of seeking the satisfaction of some common substantive want" (205). Purposive association is, according to Oakeshott, "a many speaking with one voice" where "all the tongues . . . are agreed, not merely to speak the same language, but to say the same thing" (205). Within purposive association, as Oakeshott noted, "a many become one on account of their common substantive engagement and jointly seized of complete control over the manner in which it is pursued" (205).

Assumed of as an ongoing rather than as a transitory enterprise, a purposive association may develop a formal set of rules designed to regulate the conduct of its members. The purpose of the state will not be seen here in terms of observing such rules of conduct, however. The function of any rules of conduct that exist within a purposive association is purely instrumental. They serve to elicit and to facilitate individual actions in pursuit of the common purposes of the state. They are, as Oakeshott noted, "devices favorable to the prosecution of the joint enterprise" (1975, 205). Such rules, where they exist, are "instrumental rules whose desirability lies in their propensity to promote, or at least not to hinder, the pursuit of the purpose" (1991, 451).

In this regard, a purposive association or state would seem to resemble closely what Michael Polanyi has termed a "corporate" or a "planned" social order, that is, a "method of establishing order" that "consists in limiting the freedom of things and men to stay or move about at their pleasure, by assigning to each a specific position in a prearranged plan" (1941, 431). Friedrich Hayek has written likewise of the idea of a social order as a "taxis" or a "made" order, one that is "designed for the achievement of particular ends or a particular hierarchy of ends" (1978, 75). Polanyi's and Hayek's definitions are useful here in drawing our attention to an additional characteristic of purposive association. In particular, a purposive association is characteristically one that has been consciously designed, or at least consciously adapted, by some individual or group of individuals to attain a particular set of substantive purposes deemed to be desirable.

As a vision of the state, purposive association draws on what is a very familiar form of human association, one of managed cooperation toward some common substantive ends or objectives. Businesses, unions, churches, schools, professional associations, armies, political parties, and civic groups all constitute various forms of organized human association in which their members understand their actions as being related somehow to the substantive ends or interests of their organizations. What is important about the vision of the state as a purposive association, however, is that the ends of such a state must, in the final analysis, be sovereign over the ends of all other purposive associations and that such a state can tolerate the existence of other purposive associations only to the extent that their ends and activities are in harmony with its own. As Oakeshott argued, the state as a purposive association "cannot accommodate purposive associations whose purposes are eccentric or indifferent to its purpose" (1975, 316).

The reader might be forgiven here for thinking that this particular vision of the state has developed only recently in our political history, arising perhaps out of the heady optimism of the Age of Enlightenment, the French Revolution, or the utopian writings of nineteenth-century socialists. In fact, as Oakeshott (1975, 1993) makes clear, its roots in practice and thought go back for more than four centuries to the Reformation and can be seen, for example, in the development of European Calvinist states such as Geneva.

The Ends of Purposive Association

The ends that unite a purposive association can vary and have varied over history. They have included, for example, the enactment in society of what is seen as the will of some religious god or deity so as to procure the salvation of human souls. Here, the state becomes the political embodiment of a specific religious faith, and its activities, namely the regulation of the conduct and beliefs of its members, become those of a church. Alternatively, the end of the state has been seen as the promotion of the full economic development or exploitation of a community's natural and human resources. The vision advanced in this version of purposive association is that of the state as an economic enterprise of production and commerce. The state becomes a factory, as it were. Others have advanced visions of purposive association in terms of maintaining and developing the physical and mental health of a population, that is, a vision of the state as a "therapeutic" enterprise or a hospital. Isaiah Berlin captured the essence of this particular vision when he noted critically the views of those who see the problems of humankind as "tensions (within or between individuals or groups or nations) that need to be released, wounds, conflicts, fixations, 'phobias' and fears, psychical and psycho-physical abnormalities of all sorts which require the aid of specialized healers—doctors, economists, social workers, teams of diagnosticians or engineers or other masters of the craft of helping the sick and the perplexed" (1969, 34–35). Still others have sought a state dedicated to the eradication of poverty, to the attainment of a more just distribution of goods and services among members of the community, or to the promotion of some sort of identifiable ecological balance between the needs of human civilization and nature. Oakeshott himself captured the variety of ends possible within a vision of purposive association when he argued that it has been in the past a "vision of a state as a development corporation, its members related to one another as 'workers' in a collective undertaking devoted to the maximum exploitation of its resources and managed by a board of directors" but has "displayed itself also in temporary expedients to promote affluence or diminish poverty and in bursts of missionary zeal toward the world at large" (1991, 452–453).

Perhaps the most common substantive end to which most states have dedicated themselves at one time or another is the prosecution of full-scale war against some real or imagined enemy. In fact, it is during major wars, particularly those of the past century, that we have seen states acting most purely in the fashion of a purposive association. At such times, a large portion if not all of the human and physical resources within the territory of the state are systematically and centrally directed, according to a plan, for the accomplishment of military victory. Also, it is during wartime that we expect that the ends, interests, dreams, hopes, and even lives of citizens should be sacrificed to the ends of the state. Especially in the twentieth century, wars have led to the more or less complete imposition of a military model of purposive association on the state. For the members of the state, wars have become, as Oakeshott noted, "occasions for the almost total mobilization, management, and direction of their attention, their energies and their resources in pursuit of a single purpose" (1975, 273). Lionel Robbins, a prominent economist defending British collectivist policies in World War II, has similarly argued that "in total war there is only one prime object of policy, the achievement of total victory. To that object all other aims are subordinated, by that special criterion all special operations must be judged. Whatever may be the outcome of victory . . . if the alternative is annihilation, then, while the will to survive persists at all, no sacrifice seems too great. What is to come after does not matter; if there is no victory there is no future" (1947, 47).

What these different visions of a purposive state have in common is that human activities within the state are seen as ideally directed toward the cooperative accomplishment of something that is substantive. The ends of a purposive association can never be those of simply establishing conditions seen as necessary for individuals to achieve their own particular diverse ends and values. What is required, rather, is that individuals conform their own actions and their own ends to the achievement of a common shared end or set of ends. In this regard, therefore, whereas the direction of human effort either to "increasing the economic wealth of the community" or to assuring "a more equal distribution of wealth" among individuals might constitute possible ends for purposive associations, the specification of general conditions helpful to the pursuit of diverse individual ends, conditions such as "liberty," "peace," or "public tranquility," would not themselves constitute such ends. According to Oakeshott, the "common good" in purposive association is not to be understood "in terms of tolerating the activities and choices of the individuals who compose the society, but as a comprehensive pattern of conduct imposed on all subjects alike" (1993, 89).

In characterizing the various possible ends of purposive association, it is important to understand that such ends are not always laid out by their proponents in any explicit or well-defined fashion. Instead, such ends or outcomes are often merely hinted at or are implied in the character of political discourse and practice. As Oakeshott observed, such ends may be "clearly or somewhat vaguely imagined" and "precisely or somewhat roughly specified" (1975, 264). They may be "recognized as substantive conditions of things to be achieved and enjoyed in a near or a distant future" or as "an enduring common interest to be continuously explored and promoted" (264). What is characteristic of a vision of purposive association, however, is that one can at least discern a general outline of some substantive condition of things that are to be sought on behalf of the community and that this condition is seen as representing, in the final analysis, the justification for all political action.

The Government of Purposive Association

A vision of the state as a purposive association implies its own particular kind of government. Within such an association, the engagement of government will be recognized as that of a "manager" of a corporate enterprise or collective. Its task as manager of the state is to articulate and to specify in operational terms what are the substantive ends of the state and then to deploy human and physical resources for the accomplishment of those ends. Government here takes for itself a prominent aspect of "lordship" in that it is understood that the physical and human resources of the state constitute, in a real sense, some sort of an "estate" to be managed at its discretion and in accordance with its desires. According to Oakeshott, the role of government within purposive association is "to determine, to choose the pattern of activities, the condition of human circumstance to be imposed upon its subjects, to choose the 'common good,'" and to organize "the activities of its subjects so that each shall make a specific contribution to the achievement of the condition of human circumstance believed to be 'good'" (1993, 91). Government is teleocratic, "the management of a purposive concern" (Oakeshott 1975, 205–206).

Within such a vision of government, politics, defined in terms of the resolution of conflicting interests, values, or ends, disappears. Politics becomes simply about the application of power over men, women, and things to accomplish the ends of the state. Those political disputes that do arise will take the form of disagreements to be resolved with respect to how best to pursue these ends. In other words, within purposive association, the only meaningful political questions are questions about means or about instruments. This was seen by Berlin, who was himself quite critical of this view of politics. Berlin argued, with a deliberate sense of irony, that "if we could construct a society in which it was believed universally . . . that there was only one overriding human purpose: for example, a technocratic society dedicated to the single end of the richest realization of all human faculties; or a utilitarian society dedicated to the greatest happiness of men; or a Thomist or communist or Platonic or anarchist, or any other society which is monistic in this sense—then plainly all that would matter would be to find the right roads to the attainment of the universally accepted end" (1979, 150).

Michel Foucault also seems to capture much of the meaning of teleocratic government, in its modern context, in his idea of "governmentality," which he believes characteristic to a degree of all modern states. Governmentality, according to Foucault, is the idea of a government as "a right manner of disposing things so as to lead to . . . an end which is 'convenient' for each of the things that are to be governed" (1991, 95). From this perspective, "with government it is a question not of imposing law on men, but of disposing things . . . to arrange things in such a way that, through a certain number of means, such and such ends may be achieved" (95). In Foucault's view, governmentality has come to mean a government that "has as its purpose not the act of government itself, but the welfare of the population, the improvement of its condition, the increase of its wealth, longevity, health, etc." (100). Furthermore, the population not only defines the purposes of government in terms of its needs and aspirations but also serves as an instrument to accomplish those objectives. The population is, as Foucault observed, both "the end of government" and an "object in the hands of the government" (100).

Furthermore, in addition to its managerial and instrumental character, government within a purposive association is also characterized by a certain readiness or a willingness to exert its power. Because power is the necessary instrument by which the desired ends of the state are to be secured, there will be little worry or embarrassment on the part of government in regard to the exercise of power. Concentration of political power will be seen here as facilitating the efficient and effective accomplishment of state purposes and, therefore, will be seen as desirable. Consequently, there will be little patience with the type of constitutionalism that is understood, in the English and American sense, as a means or a set of devices for dispersing power or checking the abuse of power. Rather, such constitutional devices as a separation of powers, judicial review, or federalism will be seen essentially as little more than impediments or obstacles to the pursuit of state ends. It will be thought necessary and desirable here that power should not be fragmented but instead centralized so as to permit government to pursue state purposes in a fashion that is both effective and efficient.

A state conceived as a purposive association might be thought of as entailing a highly authoritarian form of government or even a dictatorship. To think along such lines, however, would be to conflate two quite different political questions. The idea that a state should be a purposive association determines the tasks or the undertakings of its government. In other words, it determines choices with respect to what things government will do and how it will do them. It does not determine, however, who it is who will make such choices. In this regard, questions about "who shall rule?" should be distinguished from questions about "what shall government do?" As Oakeshott observed, "What we are disposed to believe or approve in respect of the authorization and constitution of government neither favors nor obstructs (much less compels or excludes) any particular disposition in respect of the pursuits of government" (1993, 9). This distinction is important because, as will be seen later, although the idea of the state as a purposive association has been encouraged by the practices of powerful absolutist monarchs such as Frederick the Great, many advocates of this idea, especially in the United States, have often made clear their opposition to authoritarianism and their deeply held commitment to democracy as a form of government.

A Comparison with Civil Association

The nature of this vision of purposive association can perhaps be better understood by briefly comparing it with what has been its chief competitor, as a vision of the state, since the end of the Middle Ages. This alternative vision is a vision of what Oakeshott (1975, 1991) termed "civil association." A civil association is one in which men and women see themselves as essentially free to pursue their own particular interests and values. What is understood to bind them together as a political group is not any common set of substantive ends or objectives. Rather, they understand themselves as bound together by their recognition or their acknowledgement of certain rules of conduct. Such an association is, in Oakeshott's words, "a relationship in terms of noninstrumental rules of conduct . . . not rules that specify a practice or routine purporting to promote the achievement of a substantive purpose" (1991, 454). These rules of conduct serve to limit individuals' spheres of action and, in doing so, limit conflict between individuals and groups and the harm that they can do to each other. As Oakeshott noted, the rules of a civil association are like "the rules of a game which are directions, not about how to win but about how to play, or the rules of public debate, which do not tell a speaker what to say and are wholly indifferent to any particular conclusion" (1991, 454).

We shall examine more fully this alternative vision of the state later on in this book. Suffice it to note for now that both visions have shaped Western political thought, discourse, and practice. What is important to understand, however, are the similarities and differences between the visions of civil association and purposive association. What the visions of purposive and civil association clearly have in common is that both seek to define an understanding of the terms of engagement of individuals with each other and with their government. In other words, both propose a form of social order or cooperation among individuals.

In this sense, both can be contrasted with an anarchical or an atomistic vision of society. What distinguishes the vision of purposive association from that of civil association, however, is the idea in the former that the activities of individuals in the state must be organized around the pursuit of a coherent set of substantive ends. To the extent that individuals engage in actions to promote their own substantive ends or those of organizations and groups, these actions are tolerated within a purposive association only to the degree that they also promote or, at the very least, do not interfere with the promotion of the substantive ends of the state. A civil association, in contrast, has no substantive ends as such, and individual or group actions are seen as directed toward achieving their own particular substantive ends. To the extent that a civil association may be said to have any ends of its own at all, such ends are not substantive and may be said to consist in simply resolving, by means of rules, the various conflicts or collisions that occur between the different ends and values of different individuals or groups in the state. In other words, whereas a purposive association may be conceived of as a purpose-based order, a civil association is more accurately defined as a rule-based order.

Advocates of Purposive Association

The idea of the state as a purposive association has not been without its advocates among philosophers. Leaving aside the classical philosophers, we can find perhaps one of the earliest philosophical expressions of a vision of a purposive state in the writings of Sir Francis Bacon in which he lays out his own ambitious agenda for science in the service of humanity. For Bacon, the destiny of humankind was the mastery of nature and the exploitation of its resources. As Bacon noted, "Man is but the servant and interpreter of nature" (1939a, 22), and humankind's ambition or purpose should be "to establish and extend the power and dominion of the human race itself over the universe" (1939b, 86). He called on the human race to "recover the right over nature which belongs to it by divine bequest, and let power be given it; the exercise thereof will be governed by sound reason and true religion" (1939b, 86). The political character of this vision emerges, perhaps most explicitly, in Bacon's *Atlantis*, a fictional account of a utopian community guided by an elite house of scientists, inventors, and discoverers whose end is "the knowledge of causes, and secret motions of things; and the enlarging of the bounds of human empire, to the effecting of all things possible" (1942, 288).

This vision of a purposive state is even more fully articulated in the early nineteenth century in the work of the French philosopher Henri De Saint-Simon and his followers. For Saint-Simon, "The main effort [of the community] should be directed to the improvement of our moral and physical welfare" (1964, 76). In order to accomplish this end, Saint-Simon advocated giving "priority in State expenditure to ensuring work for all fit men, to secure their physical existence; spreading through the proletarian class a knowledge of positive science; ensuring for this class forms of recreation and interests which will develop their intelligence" (77). These efforts were to be administered by those "most fitted to manage the affairs of the nation, . . . [its] scientists, artists, and industrialists" whose work "contributes most to national prosperity" (78).

For the followers of Saint-Simon, the high points of human history were what they termed the "organic periods," those periods when "the goal of activity is clearly defined" and "all efforts are dedicated to achieving this goal" (Iggers 1972, 53). These philosophers argued that "we are marching toward a world where . . . duty and interest, theory and practice, far from being at war, will lead to the same goal, to the moral elevation of man; and where science and industry will daily have us know and cultivate the world" (56). They saw Saint-Simon as showing "the definitive goal towards which all human capacities must converge: the complete abolition of antagonism and the attainment of universal association by and for the constantly progressive amelioration of the moral, physical, and intellectual condition of the human race" (79).

Purposive Association and Science

As the discussion above indicates, a vision of a state as a purposive association has often, although not always, been associated with an optimistic view of the sciences, both physical and social. That this should be so should hardly be surprising. A vision of a purposive political association would, after all, seem to presume the existence of knowledge, scientific knowledge in the modern context, with which individual actions can be harnessed toward the attainment of certain concrete ends or results sought by the state. Indeed, absent the existence of some sort of religious or transcendental insight, it is difficult to see how one could possibly sustain a belief in the viability of purposive association in a large complex social order unless one also was prepared to believe that scientific knowledge could somehow reveal the connection between particular human actions and particular ends of the state.

Furthermore, as we have seen earlier, political questions within a purposive state are defined not in terms of how to seek to reconcile conflicting values and ends but in terms of selecting the means necessary to achieve a coherent set of state ends. It is perhaps only natural that those who are committed to such a vision of governance should then look to scientists and technologists to help them identify the most efficient and effective means of attaining state purposes. As Berlin observed, within such a vision,

> to find roads is the business of experts. It is therefore reasonable for such a society to put itself into the hands of specialists of tested experience, knowledge, gifts and probity, whose business it is, to use Saint-Simon's simile, to conduct the human caravan to the oasis the reality and desirability of which are recognized by all. In such a society, whatever its other characteristics, we would expect to find intensive study of social causation, especially of what types of political organisation ... are best at advancing society towards the overriding goal (1979, 152).

Finally, what the vision of the state as a purposive association and optimism regarding science in human affairs both have in common is a strong faith in the powers of reason. They reflect what I have termed elsewhere a "rationalist worldview" (Spicer 1995). Because of this faith in the powers of reason, those who tend to be optimistic about the ability of men and women to work cooperatively through government for common purposes or ends also tend to be optimistic about the ability of science and experts to provide guidance in this regard.

It should be noted that the vision of purposive political association is often related not simply to a faith in science in general but also to faith in a particular kind of science. If we accept that the state can be thought of as seeking certain substantive ends, then science will often be seen primarily as an instrument for the accomplishment of those ends. Its role, therefore, will become one of providing suitable or efficient and effective techniques or technologies for the accomplishment of the ends of the state rather than the generation of knowledge for its own sake. After all, if individuals are related in terms of a set of substantive ends, then the value of their actions, even those of scientists, will be seen in terms of their contribution to the attainment of those ends. This instrumental view of science is illustrated most clearly, as Polanyi has shown, in the case of totalitarian states, where "pure" science, as distinct from scientific technology, is often attacked and where science is seen as arising "in response to the specific practical needs of contemporary society" (1941, 428).

It is worth noting in this regard the close link between the development of modern social science and American political and social reform movements of the later nineteenth century, which urged a more aggressive role by government in dealing with economic and social problems. James Smith has described this alliance between social scientists and reformers. He notes the development of the American Social Science Association after the Civil War as an "umbrella organization" for social scientists, reformers, and government officials. According to Smith, for members of this group, "social science, reform, and notions of Christian charitable obligation were virtually synonymous. They all considered themselves scientists in some respect, duty bound to investigate society's most troublesome conditions, and they assumed that science held the key to social remedies" (1991, 27). These reformers and scientists were convinced that, with the aid of social scientific knowledge, government could be used more aggressively as a tool to solve the problems and ills of an increasingly urban and industrialized society.

The American Economic Association was born out of a similar reformist zeal. Its constitution, drafted in 1887 by Richard Ely and other reform-minded economists, declared that government was "an agency whose positive assistance is one of the indispensable conditions of human progress" and that "the progressive development of economic conditions" required "a corresponding development of legislative policy" (American Economic Association 1887, 35–36). It called for "the united efforts . . . of the church, of the state, and of science" in providing solutions to "a vast number of social problems" (36). What is conveyed here is an image of social science in the service of important and substantive state ends. Ely himself hoped that the association would aid in "the development of a system of social ethics" in which we would hear "more about duties and less about rights" (American Economic Association, 1887, 17). He believed that the association should emphasize "the mission of the State and the mission of the individual in that State" (17).

Purposive Association and Administrative Power

Although the writings of political philosophers and theorists, reformers, and economists may be helpful in highlighting or sharpening up some of the intimations of a vision of purposive association, it is important to understand the practical aspects of this vision. In particular, it is clear that the implementation of a vision of purposive association requires that government be in a position to exercise a considerable amount of power over the resources and the activities of its subjects. The existence of substantial power in the hands of those who govern is required for the direction and coordination of physical and human resources by government in servicing whatever substantive ends are sought by the state. Without it, a political vision of purposive association would likely remain simply a dream.

A crucial element here, at least for any social order of a certain complexity, is the availability of a powerful administrative apparatus. Such an apparatus will be seen as required in order to inform subjects of those specific actions that are expected of them and to inspire, persuade, and, if necessary, coerce them into undertaking these actions. An administrative apparatus is also required as an instrument of intelligence to collect information concerning the existing condition and disposition of both the physical and human resources of the state so that government can assess the progress being made toward achieving state ends and then take whatever corrective measures are seen as necessary. Finally, an administrative apparatus is required as a source of technical expertise so that the ends of the state may be pursued in the most effective and efficient manner possible.

In light of these requirements, it might be thought that the first order of business within a purposive association would be the development of a large and powerful administrative apparatus. From this perspective, public administration, as we have come to know it, might be seen logically then as the product or creation of a vision of purposive association. Oakeshott's writings, however, suggest that such an interpretation would be misleading in historical terms. In his view, it has been the increased availability of power, both political and administrative, that has helped prompt the emergence of different visions of purposive association rather than vice versa. In Oakeshott's view, "What a government does, and what it may be expected to do, and even what it may be thought proper for it to do or to attempt, are conditioned by the resources of power it already commands or plausibly hopes to command" (1993, 10).

To put it another way, without the existing availability, or at least the potential availability, of a considerable amount of government power over persons and things, it is not only far more difficult to run a state as a purposive association but also far more difficult even to imagine or conceive of a state run along such lines. As Oakeshott observed, prior to the sixteenth century, "the main circumstance that prevented the activity of governing's being, or being thought proper to be, an activity of enterprise was . . . the conspicuous lack of power to be enterprising" (1993, 10).

In light of this perspective, it may be useful, therefore, to examine briefly the increase in administrative power that began to take place starting around the late fifteenth and early sixteenth centuries. Most students of history are, of course, aware that there was, during this period of time, a substantial centralization and monopolization of political power by the monarchs of the emerging nation states of Europe. Kings, queens, and princes sought systematically to expand their power over their territories at the expense of other competing institutions, including the church, the Holy Roman Empire, and the local aristocracies (Dyson 1980). Nevertheless, what also clearly began to emerge, starting in the sixteenth century, and what developed substantially across the next two centuries, was an increasingly powerful administrative machine available to the rulers of Europe. Indeed, it may surprise the modern reader to learn that a large amount of the administrative technology that we normally associate with contemporary government was already available or about to become available to the governments of the sixteenth century. As Oakeshott observed, "Almost the whole apparatus by means of which governments in our own day are able to exercise a minute control over the activities of their subjects—the apparatus of banking and bookkeeping, the records, registers, files, passports, dossiers and indexes—was already waiting to be exploited" (1996, 50). The agents of this apparatus included, in Oakeshott's words, "constables, comptrollers, surveyors, prefects, commissioners, proctors, wardens, superintendents, inspectors, overseers, collectors of informa-tion, and officials of all kinds, together with their assistants, their Bu-reaux, Boards, Commissions, Committees, Conferences, etc." (1975, 267).

In short, the administrative apparatus of sixteenth-century govern-ment comprised many of the features of what we have come to know today as the "bureaucracy." Without its availability, the centralization of monarchial power that took place in the sixteenth and seventeenth centuries would simply not have been possible. This apparatus gave government, as Oakeshott argued, "the ability to act quickly, economi-cally, with effect and with certainty" by making possible a "high degree of mastery over men and things" (1996, 50–51). In doing so, it also made it easier both for rulers and for political writers to begin to think about a state in terms of a purposive association. I do not mean to suggest here that the availability of administrative power somehow caused, on its own, states to take on the character of a purposive asso-ciation. Rather, as Oakeshott observed, this increase in administrative power, along with other developments, "merely nourished this reading of their character and provided rulers, if they were so disposed, with opportunities to move in this direction or reduced the hindrances which stood in the way of their doing so" (1975, 267).

Administrative Surveillance and Control

Across the next few centuries, additional refinements in administra-tive technology increased still further the power available to govern-ment. Perhaps one of the best descriptions of this developing technology of administrative power has been provided in the historical work of Foucault (1977, 1980, 1988). Foucault described in rich detail how, from the seventeenth and eighteenth century on, both government and private organizations were able to develop, to refine, and to put into practice more effective disciplinary techniques for the surveillance and control of human activity in large groups. His writings show how such superficially mundane and innocuous practices as the design of archi-tecture and physical space, space assignments within buildings, rank assignments, classification tables, timetables, schedules, instruction manuals, command signals, training exercises, organizational hierar-chies, performance standards, penalties and rewards, and examinations and investigations were all combined into a system of social control.

This system of control, although more subtle, more private, and less violent than that exercised in earlier times, was at the same time both more extensive and more efficient. Also, equally important, such techniques of control, because of their subtlety, were less likely to provoke opposition from those who were its subjects than more direct and violent instruments of coercion.

What developed, Foucault argued, was "a whole technique of human dressage by location, confinement, surveillance, the perpetual supervision of behavior and tasks, in short, a whole technique of 'management'" (1988, 105). This system of control made itself felt not only within prisons, armies, schools, and police agencies but also within hospitals, workshops, and factories. It provided what Foucault termed a "discipline of the minute" applied to the individual where "every detail is important" and where there is "supervision of the smallest fragment of life and of the body" (1977, 140). It ensured, as Foucault argued, the "circulation of the effects of power through progressively finer channels, gaining access to individuals themselves, to their bodies, their gestures and all their daily actions" so that "power, even when faced with ruling a multiplicity of men, could be as efficacious as if it were being exercised over a single one" (1980, 151–152).

For Foucault, the architectural metaphor or image for this type of political and social power was that of the "panopticon," literally a type of prison building proposed by Jeremy Bentham. Such a prison consists of a ring-shaped building in the center of which sits an observational tower from which a supervisor can, with the assistance of strategically placed windows, see the activities of prisoners in all of the rooms located along the ring of the building. Panopticism, as a general principle of disciplinary power, refers to an economical form of generalized social surveillance and control whereby the few can watch the many who, in turn, are constantly aware that they are being watched by the few. Within such a panoptic system of control, Foucault argued, "you have the system of surveillance which . . . involves very little expense. There is no need for arms, physical violence, material constraints. Just a gaze. An inspecting gaze, a gaze which each individual under its weight will end by interiorising to the point that he is his own overseer, each individual thus exercising this surveillance over, and against, himself . . . power exercised continuously and for what turns out to be a minimal cost" (1980, 155).

What Foucault has provided us with here is a vivid picture of how, with the availability of increasingly powerful devices and techniques of administration, various human organizations became able to exercise an unprecedented degree of control over people and things. These "methods of administering the accumulation of men" enabled what Foucault termed "a political take-off" by replacing "traditional, ritual, costly, violent forms of power" with a "subtle, calculated technology of subjection" (1977, 220–221).

Foucault's objective was to show us how these devices and techniques enabled disciplinary power to permeate and be present constantly throughout society. What is important to observe, however, is that this emerging administrative technology was available to governments of the time and was drawn on by them. Although at least initially government rulers typically saw these technologies as simply a means to repel foreign enemies more effectively, to collect taxes, and to maintain public order, they provided growing encouragement for the development of a much more ambitious agenda for governance. They seemed to render feasible what previously could be scarcely even imagined—a large powerful state in which the efforts of literally millions of individuals engaged in a variety of different activities could be somehow directed toward a common substantive end or set of ends.

Certainly, one sees, from the sixteenth to the eighteenth century, that the activities of government began slowly to expand and that they began to take on more and more the character of that of a manager of a purposive association, particularly within continental Europe. This is evidenced in the increasingly detailed regulation by government of agriculture, industry, mining, and domestic and international trade typical of the seventeenth century, a system of regulation that came to be known as mercantilism. The vision of purposive association became even more evident, however, when in the eighteenth century, responding to a large increase in population, government began to take on even greater responsibilities for the management of the details of the lives of its subjects. Men and women came to be seen by their rulers not simply as subjects to be subdued or placated but rather as resources to be cultivated and employed in the pursuit of important government purposes, including the military protection and expansion of national territories and the generation of economic wealth. As Foucault argued, population became seen as a set of problems to be managed, investigated, and controlled. According to Foucault, "The great eighteenth-century demographic upswing in Western Europe, the necessity for co-ordinating and integrating it into the apparatus of production and the urgency of controlling it with finer and more adequate power mechanisms cause 'population,' with its numerical variables of space and chronology, longevity and health, to emerge not only as a problem but as an object of surveillance, analysis, intervention, modification, etc." (1980, 171).

Again, it must be admitted that this expansion in the scope of government activity was often not prompted, initially at least, by any grand vision of purposive association. It was more often a result of the concerns of rulers simply to provide an adequate defense, to raise needed tax revenues, and to maintain public order. Nonetheless, especially as the Age of Enlightenment began to take hold of the imaginations both of rulers and of philosophers, the growing scope of governmental power seemed to provide confirmation of the possibility of the practice of government as a teleocracy and the practice of politics as a purposive association.

Summary

In this chapter, I have sought then to describe in some detail a vision of the state as an organization or as an enterprise dedicated to the pursuit of some substantive end or set of ends such as the salvation of human souls, economic development, or economic and social justice. The role of government as the manager of such an enterprise has also been explored. Furthermore, I have argued here that this vision of the state has been significantly encouraged by a substantial increase in the amount of administrative power available to governments in the modern era. Again, I would not suggest that an increase in administrative power, on its own, caused the development of the idea of a purposive state. Rather, as Oakeshott put it, this increase in administrative power, along with other factors, simply "enhanced its plausibility" (1975, 267). In this sense, the history of administrative practice and of purposive association, as a vision of the state, has been intimately connected for several centuries or more.

If this analysis is correct then, it renders all the more plausible the thesis of this book that American public administration as a field reflects, in significant part, a vision of a purposive association. No doubt some will think that I have exaggerated the relationship between developments in administrative practice and the emergence of a vision of the state as a purposive association. They might argue that many of the developments in administration discussed above were necessary for the development of any sort of nation-state, and that, in this sense, such developments helped foster a variety of visions of the state including the vision of purposive association. The latter point is, in my view, essentially correct. Without a government with sufficient administrative power to defend state borders and to enforce state laws, any idea of a group of people or a territory as a state is difficult to imagine. My argument, however, is that developments in administrative practice provided especially strong encouragement for the vision of purposive association. In order to demonstrate more clearly this connection between administrative practice and political thought, in the next chapter I will examine more closely the example of the practice and philosophy of politics and administration in eighteenth-century Prussia.

3
The Prussian Experience and the Purposive State

In the last chapter, I argued that the development and use of a powerful apparatus of administration helped foster a vision of a purposive state and a teleocratic government. One important example of how this fostering has occurred can be seen in the experience of eighteenth-century Prussia under the rule of Frederick the Great, the most well-known and influential of the so-called enlightened despots of modern Europe. Although it was Frederick's father, Frederick William I, who must really be credited with the development of the Prussian administrative apparatus, it was Frederick arguably who used this apparatus to most effect. Influenced by Enlightenment scholars, Frederick was among the first of the European monarchs to think of himself self-consciously as the head of a nation-state, as opposed to simply a ruler of a piece of territory owned by him, and he used his bureaucracy in a purposeful and aggressive fashion for the enhancement of state interests and power. The Prussian bureaucracy under Frederick the Great may be seen from this perspective as, in many ways, a prototype of the modern administrative state.

In this chapter I will look at how Frederick governed the Prussian state and how he administered his bureaucracy. I will examine not only Frederick's practices but also the vision of the state that was used to justify or rationalize these practices. Following this discussion, I will trace the impact of the Prussian experience on subsequent political and social thinking. This chapter argues that, whatever were the motives of Frederick and his administrators, the example of the Prussian experience under Frederick was important in that it helped foster a faith, both within Germany and outside, in the possibilities of purposive association and teleocratic governance.

I am not denying here the importance of earlier historical experiences in shaping our ideas about the modern state (Strayer 1970; Poggi 1978; Dyson 1980). Especially noteworthy, for example, is the experience of seventeenth-century France under the absolutist rule of Louis XIV and Cardinal Richelieu (Church 1969). We should pay special attention to Frederick's Prussia, however, because here, as compared with Louis XIV's France, existed a clearer idea of the state as an impersonal entity, distinct from the personality of the ruler himself. As Gianfranco Poggi has argued, in eighteenth-century Prussia, "the state was made transcendent over the physical person of its head through the depersonalization and objectification of its power" (1978, 76). This idea of an abstract impersonal state was reinforced by the extensive apparatus of Prussian administration, which was considerably more developed than that of the French. As Poggi observed, "Frederick William I and his successor [Frederick the Great] ruled through, at the center of, a much larger, more elaborately constructed and regulated body of public organs engaged in administrative activities that were more continuous, systematic, pervasive, visible, and effective than anything Louis XIV had ever contemplated" (1978, 74).

A focus on the Prussian experience, therefore, may be useful in understanding how our ideas about the state have developed. In looking at eighteenth-century Prussian governance and administration, I draw on three different sets of sources of information. First, I will examine accounts of the practice of Prussian governance and administration provided by historians, most especially, although not exclusively, the classic descriptions of eighteenth-century Prussian bureaucracy provided by Walter Dorn (1931, 1932a, 1932b). Dorn's detailed description of the workings of eighteenth-century Prussian bureaucracy, which is based on an extensive series of German documents and interpretation of internal Prussian administrative practice, is considered by many historians to be a classic in this field. Second, I will discuss the writings of Frederick the Great himself to see how Frederick rationalized or sought to make sense of his practices and those of his administrators, both to himself and to the world at large. Frederick's writings are important to look at because, despite the long-standing controversy over Frederick's record and motives as an enlightened despot, these writings have often been used by historians to give meaning to his actions. As a result, they have helped shape the way in which his practice of governance and administration has come to be seen. Finally, I will draw on the writings of Johann Heinrich Gottlob von Justi, who served under Frederick as Prussian director of mines. Justi was arguably the most prominent of the German and Austrian cameralists. The cameralists were a group of political economists and administrative theorists of the seventeenth and eighteenth centuries who, as both writers and teachers, sought to explain how public administration might best serve the interests and aspirations of their absolutist masters. Justi's writings are especially relevant in this regard because, as Albion Small argued, they give us an "accurate and detailed contemporary picture of the policy behind Frederick the Great's type of benevolent despotism," at least "as it was idealized in the minds of theorists" (1909, 458).

The focus on the cameralists here might be questioned in light of David Lindenfeld's argument that the cameralists were part of a strand of practical rather than theoretical or utopian reasoning in German thinking about the state. As Lindenfeld argues, German writers such as the cameralists "were less concerned with articulating the goals or ends of action and were more concerned with the techniques of implementation" (1997, 2). Nevertheless, although their focus was undeniably on practical techniques of policy implementation, the writings of the cameralists, as will be shown in this chapter, clearly articulated a strong vision of teleocratic governance and a purposive state.

The Practice of Prussian Governance

In looking first at historical accounts of the governance of eighteenth-century Prussia, what is most striking to the reader is that Frederick, through his bureaucracy, was able to exercise a power over his subjects that was remarkable both for its scope and for its minuteness or detail. Frederick's policies reflected, in significant part, the mercantilist orthodoxy of his time, which was concerned with ways of maximizing the inflow of gold and silver into the royal treasury through the regulation of industry and commerce, but they also revealed a characteristically Prussian thoroughness and attention to detail. As Dorn noted, Frederick's administrators "observed the movements of commerce, kept in constant touch with local merchants, superintended the fairs in the larger cities, informed themselves on the needs of consumers at home and in the neighboring states, and went out in search of markets for Prussian manufactures. There was not a phase of urban or rural life on which they did not issue regulating ordinances. They inspected the private husbandry of peasants and the shops of burghers, and reprimanded and coerced the indolent and careless" (1932a, 84–85). In

Frederician Prussia, according to Dorn, "scarcely a phase of public or private life escaped regulation" (1932b, 261). W. O. Henderson, an economic historian, has written in a similar vein of "the extraordinary vigor" with which Frederick's economic policies were carried out (1965, x). As Henderson has observed, "The establishment of new villages peopled with foreign immigrants, the extension of farmland by draining fens and improving wastes, the expansion of existing industries, . . . the introduction of new branches of manufacture, the stimulus given to the fisheries and to overseas trade—all this was done on a scale never before attempted in Prussia" (x).

The scope and the intensity of the power that Frederick and his administrators sought to exercise over the activities and lives of their subjects are reflected in the so-called Prussian Code, a legal codification of Frederick's practice of governance and administration that was prepared under his rule but ratified only after his death. With respect to agriculture, the code indicates, for example, that "every agriculturalist is obliged to cultivate his property thoroughly and economically for his own good and for that of the community in general. Therefore he may be forced by the State to cultivate his land adequately, and if he nevertheless continues to neglect it he may be compelled to cede it to others" (Barker 1916, 46–47).

What Frederick and his administrators attempted to achieve was a centrally planned and administered command economy. Notwithstanding the disenchantment with planning and bureaucratic regulation that is characteristic of our own time, the achievements of Frederick and his administration were not inconsiderable. During Frederick's reign, Prussia was transformed from one of a number of minor German kingdoms to one of the most militarily, economically, and politically powerful of the European states. By the time of Frederick's death, the territory of Prussia had been doubled, its population had been almost tripled, its army was perhaps the finest in Europe, and it had become an important and largely self-sufficient industrial power. Dorn described the achievements of the Prussian administration under Frederick in the following terms:

> It managed to support the army of a first-rate power on the resources of a third-rate state and at the same time accumulated a large reserve in the public treasury; it opened up the mining industry in Silesia and in the Ruhr District; it carried through a project for extensive internal colonization in urban and

rural districts which added upwards of 300,000 inhabitants to the sparsely popu-
lated provinces of Prussia, thus making in 1786 every fifth inhabitant a colo-
nist; it did much to introduce the improved British agricultural methods among
the backward Prussian peasantry; it liberalized the craft gilds and adapted them
to the needs of capitalistic industry while it endeavored to execute, and not
altogether without success, a comprehensive plan to industrialize an almost
wholly agricultural country (1931, 404).

Frederick, therefore, can be seen as governing his subjects and his
state in a manner that was highly aggressive and interventionist. According to several historians, his policies and their administration were
motivated primarily by the need to raise money. Dorn noted that the
"pivotal function of the Prussian bureaucracy" was to "support the growing financial needs" of the king's army (1931, 405). "All improvements
in administrative methods and the wider scope and greater intensity of
bureaucratic activity were made to serve the supreme end of producing
a maximum public revenue" (405). Hans Rosenberg, a contemporary
historian, argues in perhaps more colorful terms that Prussian administration "tended to be identical with centrally planned and systematically organized fiscal exploitation in the service of the military police
state" (1966, 40).

The Prussian Vision of the State

Frederick was certainly aware of the importance of fiscal considerations, observing that "money is like the wand of the necromancer, for
by its aid miracles are performed" (Frederick II 1789, 21). Nevertheless, as probably the most visible and certainly the most eloquent of
the European "enlightened despots," Frederick sought to cast the activities of eighteenth-century autocracy in a more favorable light. The
prince, in Frederick's words, was "only the first servant of the state"
(29). His "first sentiment" must be "the love of country, and his only
concern should be to work for the good of the state, to which he must
sacrifice his pride and all of his passions" (Frederick of Prussia 1981,
90). This "good of the state," for Frederick, required a powerful interventionist government that would pursue aggressively, on behalf of its
subjects, what it saw as their collective good. According to Frederick,
"The prince is to the nation he governs what the head is to the man,"
and "it is his duty to see, think, and act for the whole community, that
he may procure it every advantage of which it is capable" (Frederick II

1789, 15). The prince's duties, for Frederick, consisted in "an employment of his whole powers to prevent any corruption of manners," in taking "care that the provisions for the nation should be in abundance, and that commerce and industry should be encouraged," and, as "a perpetual centinel," in watching "the acts and conduct of the enemies of the state" (1789, 11). Frederick revealed in his writings the detailed nature of the government role he had in mind. In the case of agriculture, for example, Frederick believed government should, among other things, see to it that "the lands are well-cultivated," "clear such grounds as are capable of tillage," "increase the breed of sheep and cattle," and "keep storehouses abundantly furnished" (26).

Frederick's writings intimate here a vision of the state as a community of citizens organized and run as a collective by a powerful and enlightened monarch around a set of important and substantive state purposes. This vision of a collectivist or purposive state led and managed by a powerful teleocratic government was even more forcibly articulated by the cameralists. Indeed, according to Small, "the salient fact about the cameralistic civic theory was its fundamental assumption of the paramount value of the collective interests, or in other words the subordination of the interests of the individual to the interests of the community" (1909, 16). The collectivism of Justi, for example, is openly revealed in his argument that "a republic consists of a multitude of people who are combined with each other, . . . in order, with their united energies, and under a superimposed supreme power, to promote their common happiness" (Small 1909, 317–318). For Justi, "The merging of many wills into a single will is the first moral ground of republics," and "those who merge their wills must all have a common paramount purpose," which can be no other than "the common happiness of the whole state" (405).

In order to assist administrators in promoting this "common happiness," Justi offered his version of a science of domestic public administration or *"policeywissenschaft."* Such a science was to be concerned with, as Justi noted, "all measures in the internal affairs of the country through which the general means . . . of the state may be more permanently founded and increased, the energies . . . of the state better used, and in general the happiness of the community . . . promoted" (Small 1909, 440). Justi argued here that public administration or *"policey"* should be based on three principles. First, "the lands of the republic must be cultivated and improved . . . through external cultivation" and "through increase of the population" (442). Second, "increase of the products of the country and the prosperity of the sustaining system . . . must be promoted in every possible way" (442). Finally, "care must be given to securing among the subjects such capacities and qualities, and such discipline and order, as are demanded by the ultimate purpose, viz., the common happiness" (442).

The broad as well as the detailed nature of the type of government intervention that was envisaged is shown in Justi's discussion of measures directed at increasing population, a major concern of the cameralists. Such measures included seeing to it that "food supply and employment . . . are systematically made abundant," encouraging "the immigration of rich and talented people of all kinds," supporting "all means of diminishing sickness and of preventing plague," checking "drunkenness and other demoralizing vices," encouraging and regulating "surgery, midwifery, and pharmacy," and assuring the "cleanliness of cities" (Small 1909, 342–343).

Whatever the importance of fiscal motives in driving the actions of Frederick and his administrators, the writings of Frederick and Justi provided then an intimation of something considerably more ambitious. It was a vision of a powerful, enlightened, and teleocratic government that could and would organize and manage the physical and human resources of the state in the pursuit of important state ends. These ends included not only the promotion of external security and the accumulation of adequate fiscal resources but also the full exploitation of the agricultural, industrial, and human resources of the state and the cultivation of public morals. In other words, what was advanced here was a vision of the Prussian state as a purposive association. Such an interpretation of the Prussian experience is lent support by Geraint Parry, a contemporary historian, who argues that both Frederick and the cameralists articulated a vision of a "rationalist politics," which was about "the achievement of a single end" or "a few closely linked ends" rather than "the harmonization of a wide variety of ends" (1963, 182).

Finally, the Prussian vision of a purposive state is revealed perhaps most clearly in the introduction to the Prussian Code. Here, it states that "every citizen is obliged to promote the welfare and security of the community in accordance with his position and means. If the rights and duties of the individual should come into collision with the promotion of the general welfare, the rights and advantages of the individual citizen must range after the interests of the community" (Barker 1916, 162).

Administration of the Prussian Bureaucracy

Given the broad and detailed character of government intervention in the lives and activities of the Prussian people, one might suppose that Prussian administrators were to exercise a leadership role in the Prussian state. Frederick, however, sought to administer his bureaucracy in a highly centralized fashion, and he attempted, insofar as was practically possible, to eliminate any opportunities for the exercise of significant discretionary power on the part of his subordinates. Prussian administration, according to Dorn, was "rooted in the fiction that the king knows everything, that he can do everything and does everything that is done" (1931, 408). Frederick saw the function of administration not as one of decision making by subordinates on behalf of the monarchy but rather as a means of securing information from subordinates so that he himself could make the important decisions of government. As Dorn observed, Frederick believed that neither his ministers nor their administrative agencies "could be allowed any initiative as independent administrative bodies" (414). "Royal autocracy was carried to such an extreme that all important matters above the level of ordinary routine business were sent to the King for final decision" (Dorn 1932a, 78).

Harboring an intense distrust of his officials, Frederick used various devices to maintain and extend his control over their activities. There were detailed written instructions and rules for all officials, including ministers, drawn up in some cases by Frederick himself. These laid out with "pedantic accuracy every step and every precaution which the official must take in the daily performance of his duties . . . which he must observe on pain of being summarily dismissed" (Dorn 1932a, 90–91). Also, extensive documentation and reporting was required on even the smallest of administrative actions so that, as Dorn noted, "the Prussian bureaucracy possessed accurate and detailed records of every phase of its activity" (1932a, 89). Frederick also kept an eye on the activities of his officials through written correspondence with their colleagues and their subordinates, through a network of bureaucratic spies working outside the regular bureaucracy, and through secret written annual conduct reports on officials that could serve as the basis for career advancement, job dismissal, or even imprisonment without a hearing or trial (Dorn 1931, 1932a). In addition, Frederick sought to increase control over his bureaucracy by bypassing his ministers and dealing directly with their provincial subordinates, by creating new and specialized agencies directly accountable only to him, and by personally conducting annual inspection tours around his kingdom to assess for himself the state of his various projects and enterprises. Frederick, in other words, played the role of the quintessential micromanager.

Despite these various devices, however, Frederick was never quite able to exercise the type of complete control over the actions of his administrators that he really wanted. There was often, as Dorn noted, a "silent contest between the monarch and his bureaucracy" (1931, 418). According to Dorn, "Sometimes it was the result of official inertia and reluctance to deviate from the established bureaucratic routine; sometimes it was prompted by an effort to forestall or render harmless confusing orders which issued from the cabinet of the king; again it might be the result of an official propensity to interpret royal orders generously enough to suit either the circumstances or bureaucratic convenience" (1931, 418).

Dorn provided here an example of how one minister sought to conceal his inflated estimate of the colonial population of Silesia by deliberately settling colonists along the principal road that the king ordinarily traveled on his inspection tour (1931, 417). Some writers have gone as far as to suggest that Prussian administrators often gained the upper hand in their contest with Frederick (Rosenberg 1966; Johnson 1975). Hans Rosenberg, for example, has shown how the conservative Prussian nobility, dominant in the leadership of Prussian bureaucracy, was able, with "the use of forged evidence and deliberate falsehood and trickery," to thwart Frederick's attempts at agrarian reform and partial emancipation of serfs (1966, 195). Nonetheless, although acknowledging the limits of Frederick's control over his subordinates, Dorn argued that Frederick's information network was fairly effective in keeping him well informed on the activities of his subordinates. In Dorn's view, "Now and then shady facts might be cloaked by an impenetrable smokescreen of bureaucratic verbosity. Now and then the king might even become the unconscious dupe of his bureaucracy. But the fact remains that sooner or later the king discovered almost everything" (1931, 423).

G. P. Gooch, a British biographer of Frederick, noted similarly that "the idea of hiding anything from the ruler rarely occurred to servants of the state, for Frederick, like his father, was a stern master and had his eye on them all" (1990, 67). Hans Rosenberg observed likewise that, despite bureaucratic resistance to Frederick's policies, Frederick had "the last word in all matters of importance" (1966, 192).

Frederick sought to justify this highly personalized and centralized style of administration in his own writings. He warned specifically that ministers could not be trusted to govern the state without close supervision by the prince because "they have not its real good at heart" (Frederick II 1789, 13). Frederick observed that when the prince "should abandon the helm of the state" to ministers, "each having different views, no one proceeds on general plans" (12). Under these conditions, "there is no longer any comprehensive system; each pursues his own plans, and the central point, the point of unity, is lost" (13). For Frederick, it was essential that administration be under the direct supervision and control of a powerful monarch so that "as all the wheels of a watch correspond to effect the same purpose, which is that of measuring time, so ought the springs of government to be regulated, that all different branches of government may equally concur to the greatest good of the state" (13–14). Using a sports metaphor, he further argued that "all branches of the state administration are intimately tied together in one bundle: finance, politics, and military affairs are inseparable. . . . They must be steered in a straight line, head to head, as the team of horses in the Olympic contest which, pulling with equal weight and speed, covered the course and brought victory to their driver" (Frederick II 1966, 41).

By following this course, Frederick believed, a prince "will not find himself in difficulty when he must make a quick decision, for he directs everything toward his established goal" (Frederick II 1966, 41). Frederick's purposive state, in other words, was to be serviced by a passive public administration, which would act purely as an instrument of the will of an enlightened ruler. There was to be no role here for his administrators in shaping public policy. Justi expressed the similarly instrumentalist view of the cameralists on the role of public administration when he argued that "the wisdom and perfection of government" consisted in, among other things, "government by the monarch himself, through his own insight, not merely through his ministers, and the concentration of all affairs in his strong hand" (Small 1909, 424). The instrumentalist view of public administration, expressed here by Frederick and Justi, can be seen as following from their view of governance. They saw the state as organized around the accomplishment of a set of important substantive ends, which were to be articulated and implemented by a powerful and teleocratic monarchy. Given this teleocratic vision of governance, it was perfectly logical that effective and efficient pursuit of the state ends should require the absolute subservience of public administrators.

The Influence of the Prussian Experience

The Prussian experience in governance and administration provided, therefore, a powerful image of a teleocratic government led by a powerful chief executive who, by means of an administrative apparatus subservient to his will, would seek the accomplishment of important and substantive state ends. The roots of this vision of a purposive state and teleocratic governance obviously date back further in the history of political thinking than Frederick the Great (Oakeshott 1975). Nonetheless, the Prussian experience was significant in that it nourished and sustained this particular vision of the state. Oakeshott saw this significance when he argued that the type of "enlightened government" pursued by Frederick was, at that time, "the most comprehensive version of a state understood in the terms of *universitas* and of government as a teleocratic organization to have appeared since the emergence of Europe as a manifold of states" (1975, 307–308). He noted specifically that "in all that concerns the organization of enlightened government Prussia, rather than France, was and long remained the tutor of Europe" (303). Max Beloff similarly observed that "for actual methods of government it was Prussia that seemed to provide the appropriate model of government for all reforming monarchs in the second half of the eighteenth century" (1962, 111).

Certainly, it can be argued that the Prussian experience has exerted a powerful influence in this regard over the minds of more than a few important political thinkers. Such influence is, not surprisingly, especially evident in Germany where, as Gooch observed, Frederick the

Great holds "an honored place in the German Valhalla beside Luther and Goethe, Kant, Beethoven, and Bismarck" (1990, 343). Hegel, for example, wrote admiringly of Frederick that he "kept the general interest of the State steadily in view, ceasing to pay any respect to particular interests when they stood in the way of the common weal" (1956, 441). Frederick, in Hegel's view, "made for himself an entirely universal end, the well-being and good of the state, a guiding principle in his actions" (1983, 26). Such a state in its ideal form for Hegel represented the identity of personal and subjective will with a true universal will based on reason, "a community of existence" in which "the subjective will of man submits to laws" and "the contradiction between Liberty and Necessity vanishes" (1956, 39). It is worth noting here that public administration in the Hegelian state, as in the Frederician state it was modeled on, was to serve an essentially instrumental role in achieving the ends of the state. Its task was one of "merely subsuming the particular under the universal" through the "continued execution or maintenance of past decisions, existing laws, regulations, organizations for the securing of common ends, and so forth" (Hegel 1952, 188–189). Centralized control over the actions of "ministers and their officials" was to be secured through "hierarchical organization and their answerability" (Hegel 1952, 192).

Friedrich List, an influential German economist of the early nineteenth century who visited America and was well known for his advocacy of a strong government role in national economic development, was clearly impressed by Frederick's policies and administration. He called Frederick "the great King—greater by his policy in times of peace than by his successes in war" (List 1904, 68). According to List, "To every unprejudiced mind, unclouded by false theories, it must be clear that Prussia gained her title to rank amongst the European powers not so much by her conquests as by her wise policy in promoting the interests of agriculture, industry, and trade, and by her progress in literature and science; and all this was the work of one great genius alone" (1904, 68).

Writing later in the nineteenth century, Johann Bluntschli, a leading political and administrative theorist who influenced many American political writers including Woodrow Wilson, wrote that Frederick proved "by word and deed" his understanding "for the psychological life of nations and states" (1895, 77). Bluntschli saw Frederick as "the most significant representative of the modern State and the modern view of life" (54). Such a state, for Bluntschli, was "a living and therefore organized being" and not "a mere sum of citizens" (18–19). It was a "moral and spiritual organism" with a "personality" that, "having spirit and body, possesses and manifests a will of its own" (22). The public official within this state was to exhibit not only "obedience" to official and legal orders but also "fidelity" to the "political convictions" of "his superiors" (539–541). Such fidelity on the part of public officials, in Bluntschli's view, formed "the basis of the harmony and moral cohesion of the public service" (541).

Gustav Schmoller, a leading German economist of the nineteenth-century "historical school" of economics, which influenced Richard Ely and other American economists, and also an advocate for government activism and the German welfare state, was similarly inspired by Frederick's Prussia. He saw it as approaching an ideal in which "economic forces, while living for themselves should yet entirely serve the state" and in which "the state, pursuing its own ends, should at the same time place all its might and all its members in the true service of the national economy" (Schmoller 1989, 90–91). Seeking to defend the economic policies of Frederick against his critics, Schmoller stated that "the yelping curs, the men astride of principles, who did not understand him when he died, understand him and his policy no better now. They still less understand the great problem of the creation of states and national economies" (90).

Also worth noting here, especially from the point of view of public administration, is Max Weber, who saw Frederick as "the ruler of a specifically modern bureaucratic state" (1946, 198). Inspired in significant part by the Prussian experience with autocratic administration, Weber argued that "the monocratic variety of bureaucracy" was, "from a purely technical point of view, capable of attaining the highest degree of efficiency" and was "in this sense formally the most rational known means of carrying out imperative control over human beings" (1947, 337). Its development, according to Weber, was "the most crucial phenomenon of the modern Western state" (1947, 337).

Finally, Friederich Meinecke, a prominent twentieth-century German sociologist and historian, noted that "it was Frederick's State that first created the fixed and definite form within which it was possible for a mere population to become welded together into a real people and nation with its own vital will" (1962, 308). Frederick recognized, in Meinecke's words, "the State as a pre-eminent and constraining vital force, a collective entity which . . . conditioned and embraced the happiness of the subjects, of the people" (309). In Meinecke' view, "Frederick held it a very serious and sacred task to procure for his subjects the very highest measure, compatible with the requirements of his state, of earthly happiness, material welfare, intellectual awakening and moral vigour" (282). Frederick added to "what had hitherto been the narrower aim of *raison d'état*, namely the guaranteeing and strengthening of its physical power," the "other humanitarian ideal of educating the people and making them happy" (283). In doing so, Frederick, according to Meinecke, "inserted part of the philosophy of the Enlightenment into the very idea of the power-state" (283).

When taken together, the rhetoric of these writers clearly shows that the Prussian experience inspired a strong belief in Germany that a nation could be efficiently and effectively organized in the service of important and substantive state ends by a strong enlightened leader with the assistance of a powerful but essentially subservient administrative apparatus. The influence of the Prussian experience in government and administration made itself felt far beyond the boundaries of Germany, however. Henry C. Carey, a prolific and influential nineteenth-century American economist, for instance, saw in the Prussian experience an example of what could be achieved by a more organized and balanced approach to economic development. He wrote that "we find Prussia, from the days of the Great Frederick . . . to have been engaged in an effort to lead consumers and producers, capitalists and laborers, to take their places by each other's sides, thereby bringing into orderly arrangement the positives and negatives of that wonderful battery whose plates now count by tens of millions, and by whose extraordinary performances the world has recently been so much astonished" (Carey 1967, 143).

Herbert Croly, who sought to cultivate a progressive sense of American nationalism and to strengthen the role of the federal government in economic and social policy during the Progressive Era, was also clearly impressed by the example of Prussian governance and administration from the eighteenth century on. According to Croly,

> German nationality as an efficient political and economic force has been
> wrought by skillful and patriotic management out of materials afforded by

military and political opportunities and latent national ties and traditions. During the eighteenth century the Prussian monarchy came to understand that the road to effective political power in Germany was by way of a military efficiency, disproportionate to the resources and population of the Kingdom. In this way, it was able to take advantage of almost every important crisis to increase its dominion and prestige (1965, 246–247).

Albion Small, who is seen by some as the father of American sociology, also expressed his admiration for the political and administrative ideas of Prussia when he argued in 1909 that the writings of Justi and other cameralists "contain in embryo everything which has made the German system today the most effective organizer of national energy in the world" (1909, xv). An understanding of cameralism was essential, in Small's words, to an understanding of "the achievements of German collectivism" and its "sheer economy of social efficiency" (17). J. Ellis Barker, a British historian, drew extensively on the writings of Frederick to warn in 1916 of German power in the First World War. He noted, with both fear and admiration, that, as a result of the political system created by Frederick and his father, in Germany "a single will animates the whole administration of the State, . . . the whole nation acts like a single man, and every other consideration is subordinated to the national interest" (Barker 1916, 41). Barker believed that it was "not Bismarck, but Frederick" who was "the maker of the German Empire and of the German nation" (vi) and that "those who desire to learn the secret of Germany's strength, wealth, and efficiency, should therefore most carefully study the teachings of Frederick the Great" (21). Finally, in a slightly more contemporary vein, Preserved Smith, the popular American historian, wrote in the 1930s that, "in everything but in his militarism," Frederick "was the most enlightened ruler of the time; his government was the most economical, the most efficient, the most tolerant, and the most progressive then known" (1962, 335).

The Prussian administrative experience, therefore, has been a source of encouragement and, at times, even inspiration to those who see the state in purposive terms. Again, I am not denying that other historical experiences of autocratic administration, including those of France, have also been important in providing support for this vision of a purposive state and teleocratic governance. I am simply affirming the significance of the Prussian experience in this respect.

The Prussian Experience and American Public Administration

The Prussian administrative experience may well have had particular significance for American public administration. The influence of German ideas and practices on American public administration thinking in the early part of this century has been widely noted. Early public administration teachers and writers were clearly both impressed by German administrative practice and influenced by various German ideas, including those of Hegel, the eighteenth-century cameralists, German economists of the historical school such as Schmoller, and political theorists such as Bluntschli. Dwight Waldo has noted "the late nineteenth century hegira of our students to Europe, especially to German universities" and "the doubt and self-examination occasioned by German successes," which resulted in an "emphasis upon 'efficiency' as a necessary element of democracy" (1984, 13). Barry Karl has described how young American scholars, such as Henry Baxter Adams and Albion Small, "turned to Europe, and particularly Germany, for graduate studies in the old and, more importantly, the new sciences of society" and how, after returning to institutions such as Johns Hopkins and the new University of Chicago, they sought to "combine the free traditions of American democracy . . . with the standards of science and efficiency of Germany" (1963, 9–10). Frederick Mosher has observed specifically here the influence of cameralist ideas on American public administration, arguing that "in some ways, cameralism was the principal precursor of the development of public administration in the United States in the first half of the present century" (1968, 33). According to Mosher, "A number of the early American apostles of public administration had studied in Germany and were influenced by the earlier German experience with cameralism" (33).

Woodrow Wilson made quite evident his admiration for the Prussian administrative experience when he wrote that, in Prussia, "administration has been organized to subserve the general weal with the simplicity and effectiveness vouchsafed only to the undertakings of a single will" (1887, 204). According to Wilson, it was in Prussia where "administration has been most studied and most nearly perfected" (204). Wilson noted specifically that it was Frederick the Great "who, building upon the foundations laid by his father, began to organize the public service of Prussia as in very earnest a service of the public" (204). Wilson believed that the administrative experience and ideas of Prussia, along with those of France, were to help provide the basis for a new science of public administration, one that would discover "what government can properly and successfully do" and "how it can do those proper things with the utmost possible efficiency" (197). Certainly, Wilson was by no means insensitive here to the autocratic character of Prussian governance and administration. He noted that "we should not like to have had Prussia's history for the sake of having Prussia's administrative skill" and that "Prussia's particular system of administration would quite suffocate us" (207). Nonetheless, because of his belief in a clear distinction between politics and administration, Wilson was not overly concerned about the importation of Prussian political theories or ideas. He believed that "we can borrow the science of administration with safety and profit if only we read all fundamental differences of condition into its essential tenets. We have only to filter it through our constitutions, only to put it over a slow fire of criticism and distil away its foreign gases" (219).

Leonard White, writing one of the first textbooks in American public administration, looked specifically in the first chapter of his book to the German administrative experience when he argued that "the World War brought into vivid contrast the administrative methods of democratic and autocratic governments, and gave sharp criticisms of the time-honored plan of 'muddling through'" (1926, 11). Clearly impressed by the German example, he wrote that "democracies can fruitfully borrow from more highly organized administrative systems those elements which can be properly adapted to their fundamental political institutions in order to make more effective the achievement of their own purposes and programs" (7).

Conclusion

There is good reason, then, to believe that the example of the Prussian administrative experience may well have exerted an influence on early thinking in American public administration. Obviously, any direct influence of the Prussian administrative experience is difficult to determine and should not be overstated. Frankly, many factors helped to shape the early development of the field of American public administration (Waldo 1984; Stillman 1991). American corporate business, for example, seemed to many, in the early twentieth century, to furnish a useful guide as to how to organize and administer government in an effective and efficient fashion. Also important, but often overlooked today, was the impact of religion in the early upbringing of many administrative reformers (Stillman 1998). Still, the influence of the Prussian experience should not be discounted. Even if we set aside any direct influences of the Prussian administrative experience on early public administration writers, it would still have influenced American public administration, albeit in a less direct fashion, because, as we have seen, the Prussian experience made the idea of a purposive state look more attainable in the eyes of many highly influential philosophers, political thinkers, and reformers of the nineteenth and early twentieth century. In this respect, the Prussian administrative experience under Frederick the Great may well have cast a longer shadow over American public administration than is currently appreciated.

4

American Public Administration and the Purposive State

This chapter seeks to demonstrate both the longevity and the pervasiveness of the vision of a purposive state within the literature of American public administration. I begin by examining some of the early literature in American public administration, including the writings not only of those who seem to advance what has sometimes been termed the "classical" or "orthodox" approach to public administration but also of those who have dissented to varying degrees from its tenets. Following this examination, I will look to some of the more modern mainstream writings in the field, including the work of Herbert Simon and recent writers in public policy analysis and public management. Finally, I will explore the views of some contemporary critics of mainstream public administration. My purpose here is to show that, notwithstanding a wide divergence of views in public administration, a considerable amount of this literature intimates quite strongly a vision of a purposive state and of a teleocratic form of governance and administration. I emphasize here that, in asserting the power of the idea of a purposive state within American public administration, this chapter focuses on the academic literature of public administration, not on the practice of public administration. In fact, as will be shown later, much of the actual practice of American public administration would seem to intimate a rather different vision of the state than that advanced by public administration writers.

Early Public Administration Orthodoxy

Early public administration orthodoxy rested on certain core beliefs. There was a belief in the virtues of hierarchy and of centralization of power over administration in the chief executive, a belief that public administration should be cleansed of partisan politics and corruption, and a belief in efficiency as the central value of administration. Furthermore, there was a belief that there existed certain principles

for good administration that were applicable to all organizations, regardless of institutional setting, and a belief that such principles were sus-
ceptible to empirical scientific discovery and verification. Admittedly,
not all classical writers adhered to all of these principles, but their views
were sufficiently similar so that there has been a tendency to group
them together (Fry 1989).

The literature of the early orthodoxy, from its beginnings, evoked
the idea of a purposive state and a purpose-driven or teleocratic form
of governance. Dwight Waldo has observed of these early writers that
"although they profess and believe in democracy, liberty, and equality,
they have generally accepted the alternative of a planned and managed
society" (1984, 19). Woodrow Wilson, for example, saw government
and most especially public administrators as directing the activities of
the state toward the accomplishment of an ever-expanding range of
important substantive national purposes. He observed with obvious
enthusiasm how "views are steadily widening to new conceptions of
state duty," how "the functions of government . . . are also vastly mul-
tiplying in number," and how "administration is everywhere putting
its hands to new undertakings" (Wilson 1887, 200–201). "Seeing every
day new things which the state ought to do," Wilson noted, "the next
thing is to see clearly how it ought to do them" (201). Wilson wrote of
the state in clearly teleocratic terms. It was, for him, "the organ of
society, its only potent and universal instrument" (Wilson 1889, 660),
and he believed that socialists, despite their shortcomings, had "the
right end in view," namely "to bring the individual with his special
interests, personal to himself, into complete harmony with society with
its general interests, common to all" (659).

Leonard White expressed the essence of a teleocratic vision of governance when he defined public administration as "the management of
men and materials in the accomplishment of the purposes of the state"
(1926, 2). White made clear both the substantive character and the
expansive range of the purposes he had in mind when he argued for the
"acceptance of the state as a great agency of social cooperation, as well
as an agency of social regulation" (8). In White's view, the state was "an
important means by which the program of social amelioration is ef-
fected" (8). "In every direction," he noted, "the task of the modern
state is enlarging" and "the range of public administration is being extended" (9).

A vision of teleocracy is further evident in the writings of Luther Gulick. Organization, for Gulick, was about translating "the central purpose or objective of an enterprise . . . into reality" (1937a, 6–7). It was about "the development of intelligent singleness of purpose in the minds and wills of those who are working together as a group, so that each worker will of his own accord fit his task into the whole with skill and enthusiasm" (1937a, 6). Gulick argued that this sense of a "singleness of purpose" should extend far beyond the walls of government agencies and into the minds of the citizenry and its political leadership. As he observed when reflecting on the lessons learned from World War II, "Truly effective action in administration arises from singleness of purpose and clarity of policy, ardently believed in both by the leaders and by the public in all parts of the country and in all strata of society. . . . When a nation drives forward with unity of purpose, then administration can accomplish the impossible" (Gulick 1948, 117–118).

Furthermore, Gulick clearly believed that an increasingly broad range of human action in communities should be brought perhaps slowly, but inevitably, under the domain of some type of conscious and planned coordination. He saw "no limits to the effort mankind is prepared to make to render life more secure and abundant through socially enforced co-ordination" and "no need of accepting the view that there are fixed limits of co-ordination beyond which mankind can never go" (Gulick 1937a, 40–41).

Consistent with their strongly expressed vision of a purposive state, these writers also voiced a deeply held faith in the potential of social science to direct public policy and administration. We have already seen in chapter 2 how American reformers embraced the new emerging social sciences in their quest to deal with the problems and ills of an increasingly urban and industrialized society. As Waldo noted, for early public administration writers and reformers, "Science was a cult and Expert a fetish" (1984, 29). Wilson's ideal state, for example, was one in which the science of administration was to play a substantial role in guiding not just administration, narrowly defined, but also the entire process and structure of governance. Science was going to "straighten the paths" not merely of administration but also of "government" and would "make its business less unbusinesslike, . . . strengthen and purify its organization, and . . . crown its duties with dutifulness" (Wilson 1887, 201). The "object" of such an administrative science, Wilson argued, was to discover "what government can properly and successfully do" as well as "how it can do these proper things with the utmost possible efficiency and at the least possible cost either of money or of energy" (197).

Although Wilson expressed here strong support in principle for a science of administration, he left to other writers the task of working out the details of such a science. Most notable among these, without a doubt, was Frederick Winslow Taylor. Taylor's philosophy and techniques for what he termed "scientific management" drew on his own experience in industry. Nevertheless, his writings clearly expressed a bold political and social vision. In fact, Taylor's writings, perhaps more than those of any other single writer in administration, express Sir Francis Bacon's utopian vision, discussed earlier, of a state as a scientifically guided enterprise dedicated to the efficient exploitation of its natural and human resources. This Baconian vision emerges clearly in Taylor's own summary of the program of scientific management. Scientific management, for Taylor, was about

- Science, not rule of thumb.
- Harmony, not discord.
- Cooperation, not individualism.
- Maximum output, in place of restricted output.
- The development of each man to his greatest efficiency and prosperity (1998, 74).

Taylor saw scientific management here as contributing, more than any other political or social reform of his time, "toward promoting prosperity, toward the diminution of poverty, and the alleviation of suffering" (1998, 3). Furthermore, he believed that his principles of scientific management could be applied "with equal force to all social activities: to the management of our homes; the management of our farms; the management of the business of our tradesmen, large and small; of our churches, our philanthropic institutions, our universities, and our governmental departments" (iv).

Taylor's followers were often even more effusive than he in regard to the potential contributions of scientific management to governance and society. Harlow Person, for example, argued that the philosophy, principles, and techniques of scientific management could be applied to the "conservation problems of entire nations, and perhaps of an entire world" (1972, xvi). Scientific management, for these advocates, was more than just a theory of management. It was a moral, political, and social movement. As Martha Banta has noted recently of Taylor and his cohorts, although their initial aims were only "to determine the 'one best way' to increase industrial productivity" or to clarify the "vagaries of human behavior,"

> they quickly took upon themselves a far greater aim: that of bringing order, rationality, and efficiency out of the disorder, the irrationality, and the waste-fulness of their times. Not devoid of conceit, they believed that their theory-making would resolve whatever was generally ungovernable in government procedures, business enterprises, household arrangements, and the workplace, . . . as well as (why stop before tidying up everything?) the conduct of everyday life (1993, ix).

Taylor's scientific management had a profound influence on early thinking within public administration. As Waldo put it, scientific man-agement provided "many techniques and considerable philosophy to public administration," and, in some areas, the scientific management and public administration movements were, in fact, "overlapping or indistinguishable" (1984, 49). White, for example, observed how the scientific management movement had "built up the outlines of a whole philosophy of social betterment on the basis of scientific control of the productive process" (1926, 12). In White's view, "We are wholly justified in asserting that a science of management appears to be immediately before us" (15–16). Gulick was similarly optimistic. Just as the encour-agement of the physical sciences had enabled "the conquest of the natu-ral world," so the encouragement of the social sciences could be "counted upon . . . to advance scientific knowledge and control in the world of human affairs" (1937b, 195).

This vision of science in the service of a purposive state was ad-vanced enthusiastically in the administrative writings of Henry Dennison. Dennison called for "an engineering approach to the prob-lems of government" (1937, 135). The charge for political science, in Dennison's view, was to study the community "as a field of forces—psychological, biological, and physical" and to "determine the mea-sures and structure of government which can be expected to use these forces and to relate them so as to bring about development in the di-rection of the fundamental purpose adopted by and appropriate to a particular social group" (135–136).

In addition to a faith in science, the classical writers' vision of a purposive state also strongly intimated support for strengthening the power of the chief executive over the activities of administrators. Gulick, for example, one of the most ardent advocates for a more powerful chief executive, argued that the president should be seen as "the leader of the enterprise" and that his responsibilities should include "working out in broad outline the things that need to be done and the methods for doing them to accomplish the purpose set for the enterprise" (1937a, 13). For these writers, given the presumption that there existed a set of definable and consistent national purposes, it seemed only logical that the implementation of such purposes should rest in the hands of a unified executive branch under the control of a strong, enlightened president. We should note here that many of these early writers saw no conflict between a powerful chief executive and a robust democracy. To the contrary, they regarded their reforms as absolutely necessary to strengthen and to preserve democracy at a time when it seemed in particular danger. This perspective is evident in the report of the Brownlow Committee, which was established in 1936 by President Franklin Roosevelt to provide expert recommendations for executive reorganization and which consisted of Gulick and other leading experts in public administration. As Gulick and his colleagues on the committee observed, stronger presidential control over administration was necessary "to make democracy work today in our national government; that is, to make our government an up-to-date, efficient, and effective instrument for carrying out the will of the nation" (Brownlow, Merriam, and Gulick 1997, 93).

Dissenters from Orthodoxy

Many writers who took a classical or orthodox approach to public administration expressed, then, in relatively unambiguous terms the idea of a state guided with the assistance of science and led by a strong chief executive toward the accomplishment of a set of substantive state purposes or ends. Because these writers typically emphasized centralized hierarchy as the chief mechanism for controlling human behavior, the fact that many of them might conceive of a state as an association organized and managed along teleocratic lines is not altogether surprising. Interestingly enough, however, this same vision of a purposive state can also be discerned among some early writers who dissented from the orthodoxy and who were, for their part, critical of hierarchy as a primary mechanism for social control.

Mary Parker Follett, for example, clearly rejected the authoritarian and bureaucratic style of control characteristic of the classical approach, but she did not seem to reject its vision of a purposive state. Rather, she argued for a more participatory and a more democratic approach to the determination of common ends. She saw administrative and social control not in the coercive terms of hierarchy but rather in terms of a coming together or a "unity" among the different views of different individuals involved in a particular situation. For Follett, this unity in views meant "control of the situation" (1937, 167).

Furthermore, extending her vision to the economy, Follett boldly declared that "the period of laissez-faire is indeed over" and that industry should now be coordinated by planning boards "composed of the heads of the industries themselves" and "expert economists" (1937, 169). "To get our affairs in hand, to feel a grip on them, to become free," she believed, "we must learn, and practice . . . the methods of collective control" (169). On issues of politics and governance, Follett was skeptical in regard to the effectiveness of conventional democratic procedures. She sought what she believed a fuller and more substantive approach to democracy, one rooted in active citizen participation in neighborhood and occupational groups. These groups interacting with each other, Follett argued, would constitute a "moral state . . . built anew from hour to hour by the activity of all its members" (1965, 335). Out of such a system of participatory and interactive group processes would emerge not just a common will, but *the will to will the common will"* (1965, 49). Follett, drawing like many writers of her time on Hegel, argued that "true democracy" was "the finding of the one will to which the will of every single man and woman must contribute" (157).

Follett's ideas here about the need to find an integrated unity among different views, about the need for planning and collective control guided by experts, and about the importance of formulating a unified and integrated common will within the state reflect strongly the idea of a state as a purposive association. Her writings make clear, moreover, that a belief in teleocracy need not always entail support for a centralized and bureaucratic form of public administration. They express Follett's faith in the possibility of a less hierarchical and a more humane and participatory, a more communitarian, form of collectivism than that intimated by classical writers.

Such a faith is also evident in the writings of Elton Mayo, who is often credited as one of the founders of the "human relations school" within both business and public administration. Mayo is best known by students of public administration, of course, for his empirical investigations of the effects of social interaction among workers on organizational morale and performance. Mayo believed that the problems he observed in the workplace were not unique to particular work situations, however. Rather, they were attributable to what he saw as a nationwide, indeed a worldwide, "developing social disorganization and consequent *anomie*" (Mayo 1946, 165). Industrial and technological change, in Mayo's view, had destroyed "the belief of the individual in his social function and solidarity with the group" and, most important, had undermined "his capacity for collaboration in work" (159). Mayo argued that rapid economic and social change was eroding traditional social codes of conduct and that, as a result, individuals in modern industrial societies were losing "their capacity for disciplined cooperation" (158). He saw a "failure of collaborative effort within the nation," illustrated in "the developed misunderstanding between employers and workers in every civilized country" (170).

The answer to this troubling social disorganization and failure of collaborative effort, in Mayo's view, was neither a centralized socialist state nor centralized planning. What was needed instead was enlightened leadership of both public and private organizations on the part of an administrative elite, who would be properly educated and trained in the sciences of human and social behavior. As Mayo argued, "The *elite* of the several civilized powers is at present insufficiently posted in the biological and social facts involved in social organization and control" (1946, 169–170), and "we are greatly in need of an administrative *elite* who can assess and handle the concrete difficulties of human collaboration" (177). Mayo was confident here that the scientific knowledge necessary to assist such an administrative elite would be forthcoming. He expected advances in "various studies—biochemical, medical, industrial, anthropological" to "greatly increase our understanding and control of the human problems of an industrial civilization" (161).

Mayo's readiness to generalize from the problems of cooperation on particular shop floors to those of an entire society and his deeply held faith in behavioral and social science make evident the type of ideal state that he had in mind. His vision was that of a community of individuals saved from the anomie and social disintegration of an industrialized, technological society not by the formal institutions of government but by being organized into decentralized systems of cooperative effort under the leadership of a scientifically trained administrative elite. What is evoked here is the idea of a purposive state directed through more humane and enlightened administrative leadership of its private and public organizations toward both enhancing the material prosperity of its members and restoring their psychological and social health. Indeed, Mayo's work, drawing as it does on the ideas and methods of clinical psychology, often intimates quite strongly the vision of the state as a therapeutic enterprise, which was discussed earlier in chapter 2.

In summary, therefore, both those writers who advocated a centralized and hierarchical approach to public administration and some of their more prominent critics shared a similar vision of the state. Their differences lay primarily in how best to enact such a vision. The attachment of these writers to a vision of a purposive state was undoubtedly fueled in significant part by the threat of conflicts between different economic classes in an emerging urban and industrial society and later by the threats posed to peace and democracy by a combination of economic crises and the emergence of aggressive military dictatorships abroad. Nonetheless, as will be shown next, even as these threats abated, the influence of the vision of a purposive state continued to exercise a strong hold over the literature of American public administration.

Modern Public Administration Writers

In his classic work, *Administrative Behavior,* Herbert Simon set what was a distinctly teleocratic tone for a great deal of postwar mainstream public administration, as well as the emerging new policy sciences, when he wrote that "the central concern for administrative theory" should be "the rationality of decisions—that is their appropriateness for the accomplishment of specified goals" (1976, 240). Simon sees government explicitly here in teleocratic terms. For him, it is simply a particular type of "organization," whose task it is "to bring the organizational components of its parts . . . into conformity with the objectives of the organization as a whole" (200). Furthermore, public

administrators, like business administrators, are to "take as their ethical premises the objectives that have been set for the organization"
(52).

In line with this vision of teleocratic governance, Simon envisions
an important role for science here. From his perspective, "a practical
science of administration" should consist of "those propositions as to
how men would behave if they wished their activity to result in the
greatest attainment of administrative objectives with scarce means"
(1976, 253). Furthermore, also consistent with the idea of a teleocracy,
efficiency should be "a guiding criterion in administrative decision-
making" (65). The function of the public administrator, for Simon, is
"to maximize the attainment of the governmental objectives . . . by
efficient employment of the limited resources . . . available to him"
(186–187). Efficiency, of course, is an instrumental good. When applied to government, however, the notion of efficiency must presume
the existence of some set of definable and consistent purposes. Indeed,
without the existence of such a set of purposes, the whole notion of
efficiency loses meaning and becomes vacuous.

To argue here that Simon expresses a teleocratic vision of governance might, at first glance, seem at odds with his well-known emphasis on the psychological limits of individual rationality. Nevertheless,
Simon sees human organizations as providing the means in modern
society for individuals to transcend these limits and to achieve rationality at an organizational and even social level. In Simon's view, organizations can control the "stimuli" of individual decisions "so as to serve
broader ends" and integrate "individual decisions . . . into a well-con-
ceived plan" (1976, 108–109). Indeed, for Simon, organizations are
"fundamental . . . to the achievement of human rationality in any broad
sense," and "the rational individual is, and must be, an organized and
institutionalized individual" (102). He notes that organizations "determine the mental sets of the participants, they set the conditions for the
exercise of docility, and hence of rationality in human society" (101).
In short, as Sheldon Wolin has observed, from the perspective of Simon
and like-minded theorists, organization becomes "the grand device for
transforming human irrationalities into rational behavior" (1960, 380).

The continuing power of Simon's vision of teleocracy within the
field of public administration has manifested itself in a variety of ways.
It can be seen in the preoccupation of scholars over the years with a

seemingly endless variety of rationalist decision-making techniques such as program budgeting, management by objectives, policy analysis, systems analysis, management science, and strategic planning. For example, Edith Stokey and Richard Zeckhauser, authors of a text on policy analysis written in the 1970s, express a distinctly teleocratic view of the process of public policy formulation when they indicate that their approach to public policy analysis is "that of the rational decision maker who lays out goals and uses logical processes to explore the best way to reach those goals" (1978, 3). Stokey and Zeckhauser explicitly do not consider "situations in which several decision makers with conflicting objectives participate in a decision" (3). They express a confidence in the value of science in helping make public policy decisions, drawing on "analytic techniques developed in economics, mathematics, operations research and systems analysis" (3). More recently, Stuart Nagel and C. E. Teasley indicate in a similar vein that "public policy analysis is used to inform the policy maker about the likely future consequences of choosing various alternatives. As such, it often entails defining a set of goals, determining alternative strategies available to achieve them, and determining the relations between those goals and strategies in order to choose the alternative or combination of alternatives that will best achieve those goals" (1998, 507).

It is interesting to note here that this teleocratic vision of the policy process is evident even among policy writers who acknowledge the reality of political constraints on the role of analysis. Ira Sharkansky, for example, emphasizes "the pervasiveness of politics" in policy analysis, but he still ends up by advising practicing policy analysts to "define policy goals clearly" and "as simply as possible" so as to "enhance the clarity of instructions that can be prepared for administrators" (1997, 520). Although acknowledging the importance of political factors in government decision making, many of these writers would seem to endorse a role for policy analysts as what Charles Schultze has termed "partisan efficiency advocates" or "champions of efficiency and effectiveness as criteria in decision making" (1968, 101). According to this view, policy analysts can forge "links between general values and specific program characteristics . . . by determining social production functions that relate program inputs to program outputs" and "by translating general values into operationally specific objectives against which the outputs can be evaluated" (Schultze 1968, 74). In short, much of the mainstream policy analysis literature has been about developing and encouraging the use of analytical techniques of social science in the service of teleocratic governance.

This teleocratic perspective on governance can further be found among some of the newer public management writers. These writers, like the earlier dissenters from the public administration orthodoxy, tend to be critical of bureaucratic structures and processes. They often stress the desirability of more decentralized and participatory administrative structures and processes and more creative styles of leadership. Nonetheless, these public administration writers seem to hold firm and fast to a vision of teleocratic governance. Steven Cohen, for example, in a recent book targeted at practitioners, asserts that "effective public managers try to make things happen; they pursue programmatic goals and objectives by thinking and acting strategically" (1988, 13). According to Cohen, "One of the primary motivators of public employees is their desire to be involved in critical missions," and he suggests that "it is important to build on that predisposition and explicitly connect the work of your organization to important objectives" (137). Cohen's enchantment with teleocracy here is only too obvious in his assertion that "there is something thrilling about the articulation of important public policy goals" (137). John DiIulio, another prominent writer in this field, expresses much the same vision of teleocratic governance when he argues that public organizations are the "hands and feet" of "important public purposes" and that public management as a field of enquiry should search for "ways to realize public goals by the most appropriate administrative arrangements possible" (1989, 131–132). Robert Behn notes similarly that one of the "big questions in public management" is how to "motivate public employees (and citizens too) to pursue important public purposes with intelligence and energy" (1995, 319). He expresses his clear preference for a system of teleocratic governance and administration in which public managers are given "firm, clear objectives" and then allowed "a lot of discretion in how to achieve them" (322). Michael Barzelay, in a perhaps more radical vein, calls for what he characterizes as a "Post-Bureaucratic Paradigm" in public management (1994). He argues that "concepts of mission, services, customers, and outcomes are valuable because they help public servants articulate their purposes and deliberate about how to adapt work to achieve them" (1994, 457).

Finally, a vision of teleocratic governance is revealed, in recent years, by writers in what has been termed the "reinventing government movement" (Osborne and Gaebler 1993; Gore 1993; Osborne and Plastrik 1997). Such a vision is evident, as we have already seen in chapter 1, in their fervently expressed desire for a more mission-oriented and less rule-oriented form of governance and administration, in their wish that government should more closely emulate the practices of business, and in their emphasis on the importance of defining, within the political process, a clear and consistent set of goals and objectives for government policies.

Purposive Association or Simply Purposive Administration?

One might think perhaps that these modern writers are only suggesting that we see administration or organization in more purposive terms. Many of them might well argue that all they are really seeking to do is to encourage a sense of purposefulness or mission among administrators and that they are not really implying any particular vision of the state at all. In their zeal to apply a purpose-driven or a mission-driven approach to public administration across most aspects of government, however, these writers, whether intentionally or otherwise, strongly convey the message that most, if not all, of the important activities in which government engages can somehow be translated into a coherent set of operational and measurable government purposes or missions against which public administrators can be held accountable. Their forceful rhetoric has the effect of encouraging more than just a useful sense of purposefulness in administrative conduct. It fosters the inculcation of a systemwide teleocratic perspective with respect to the apparatus of governance itself. The rhetoric of some of the new public management writers is especially revealing in this regard. The quotations provided above, for example, which refer to "critical missions," "important public policy goals," and "important public purposes" clearly indicate that these authors are not just talking about the purposes of any organization. If we are to give these authors' words the respect that they deserve, what they are talking about is what they see as important collective purposes of government and of the state.

Certainly, Behn is not oblivious to the broader political import of his advice to public managers. He wants stronger leadership by public managers not just to improve organizational performance but also to better "the American system of governance" by "compensating for some of the failures of the legislature, the judiciary, and their elected chief executive" (1998, 209). Important here among these failures, for Behn, is the propensity of elected officials to "give directions [to public managers] that are ambiguous and contradictory" (214). In other words, Behn sees the political process as failing because it does not produce a clear and consistent set of state objectives. In light of this, Behn argues that public managers "should take initiative to correct the current failures of our system of governance—particularly those failures that impinge on the ability of the manager's agency to pursue its mission effectively" (221). He advocates "leadership that takes astute initiatives designed to help the agency . . . achieve its purposes today" and "create new capacity to achieve its objectives tomorrow" (220).

In arguing that modern writers often advance a vision of purposive association and teleocracy, I do not mean to assert that all of them subscribe to a well-defined, overarching set of substantive purposes for a state. Indeed, if anything, as observed by writers such as Guy Adams (1992) and O. C. McSwite (1997), the field is typically characterized by a narrow instrumental rationalism, inspired in large part by Simon, in which the task of administrators is seen as the efficient and effective accomplishment of whatever ends or objectives they might be called on to pursue. Instrumental rationalism is often employed here by public administration writers, in part, as an attempt to escape the complexities and value ladenness of political theory. This attempted escape from political theory fails, however, because instrumental rationalism itself, when applied to government, implies a particular vision of the state. To argue, as these writers do, that public administrators should select those administrative actions or policies that achieve their purposes efficiently and effectively, whatever those purposes happen to be, is to ask that we view governance and administration through the lens of teleocracy.

Furthermore, we should note here that not all modern writers have been reticent about expounding their own vision of the state as a purposive organization. Simon, for example, as we have already seen, seems to understand fully the broader political and social implications of his emphasis on rationality in organizations. He argues that, through a process of psychological identification, "organized society imposes upon the individual the scheme of social values in place of his personal motives" (Simon 1976, 218). Moreover, in his view, organizations are "socially useful" to the degree that they bring about "a correspondence between social value and organizational value" (218). In other words, for Simon, organizations provide, at least ideally, a means of subordinating the narrow personal objectives of individuals to the broader objectives not only of the organizations themselves but also of society as a whole. Lest this interpretation of Simon's writings be thought perhaps eccentric, Terence Mitchell and William Scott have argued that Simon, along with his mentor, Chester Barnard, "saw a form of corporatism as part of America's political destiny," and although not endorsing it "in a strict fascist sense," they favored a "functionally organized society," that is, one in which the large public and private organizations of the "administrative state" were "to control the individual's behavior" and "to manipulate people's motives and values" so that they would "accept as their own the organization's values" (1988, 358).

More recently, Robert Reich, a former secretary of labor and also a prominent writer in the public management area, seems among the most effusive advocates of a purposive state when he asserts that "the public manager's job" is "to help the public discover latent contradictions and commonalities in what it wants to achieve" (1988, 124). According to Reich, government leaders should engage the public in an "ongoing dialogue" in which "society defines and evaluates its collective goals, . . . examines its norms and beliefs," and "in defining its purposes . . . becomes better able to mobilize its resources and achieve its goals" (6).

Finally, Kenneth Meier clearly has a lot more than just administrative reform in mind when he expresses his frustration over what he sees as the failure of our political system "to resolve goal conflict with informed public policy" (1997, 196). Meier argues that we should consider redesigning our entire political system "to resolve rather than exacerbate conflict" and "examine the more unified political structures and the corporatist processes of many European countries" (197). In advocating such "unified political structures" and "corporatist processes," Meier makes explicit here his strong preference for a more teleocratic form of governance and administration, as well as his willingness to have us engage in radical constitutional reform in order to achieve it.

Contemporary Critical Voices

I have so far focused on contemporary writers who, for the most part, take what might be termed a "mainstream approach" to public administration. Characteristic of this approach is a general inclination to downplay conflict about political and social ends, both within public organizations and within political communities, and to focus our attention on discovering, often with the assistance of social science, more efficient and more effective ways of achieving agreed upon political ends or purposes. Over the years, this mainstream approach has drawn fire from a number of critics who have a variety of different perspectives, including those of social equity, organizational humanism, communitarianism, interpretivism, critical theory, and postmodernism. These critics often advocate more decentralized, more democratic, and more egalitarian approaches to administration and governance, ideas that seem quite antithetical, in many ways, to any notion of a purposive state. Nonetheless, some of these authors also intimate in their writings their own particular visions of a purposive state and teleocratic governance.

George Frederickson, one of the founders of the "new public administration," for example, argues that public administrators should seek "to change those policies and structures that systematically inhibit social equity" (1971, 312). In his argument, he urges upon public administrators a set of purposes that, whatever may be their intrinsic merits, are clearly substantive in character. Frederickson wants public administrators "to work for changes which try to redress the deprivation of minorities" and "to enhance the political power and economic well-being of these minorities" (1971, 311). From the point of view of new public administration, what public administrators should strive for ideally, therefore, is some sort of a redistributive state, directed at promoting greater substantive equality in income and wealth among its citizens. Furthermore, consistent with his vision of teleocracy, Frederickson expresses a strong faith in the role science will play in serving the ends of this redistributive state. He looks forward to "quantitatively inclined public-organization theorists . . . executing a model or paradigm" in which social equity will be "elevated to the supreme objective" (330). With the help of such a model, in Frederickson's view, we might be able then to "assess rather precisely the likely outcomes of alternative policies in terms of whether the alternative does or does not enhance equity" (330).

A vision of a purposive state is further evident in the writings of critical theorists. These theorists, who draw on a blend of phenomenology, psychoanalysis, and neo-Marxism, seem to urge that public administrators take on not only a political role in administration and governance but also a therapeutic one. Robert Denhardt, for example, advocates a "critical approach" to public organizations, which will be aimed at "assisting individuals . . . in discovering and pursuing their own developmental needs, even recognizing that these may sometimes be at odds with those of the dominant values of the bureaucracy" (1981, 633). A critical approach, according to Denhardt, is needed to "give priority to the developmental needs of all parties—bureaucrats and clients" and to "focus on the distortions which have prevented the true needs of individuals from being expressed" (634). Denhardt argues here that public administrators, in dealing with their staff and clients, need to take an "educative approach," one that, through a process of critical self-reflection, "seeks to assist people in determining their true needs, as well as the social conditions which prevent fulfillment of those needs" (634). Such a critical approach, in Denhardt's view, can help reveal what Habermas terms "'the false consciousness' which binds us, thus permitting movement toward emancipation" (631).

Bayard Catron and Michael Harmon, in a similar vein, call on public administration theorists to "begin, through collaborative or therapeutic modes to assist administrators in breaking *their* conspiracy against clients" (1981, 540). According to Catron and Harmon, the role of the theorist as therapist would be to assist "actors in the administrative process, including administrative actors, politicians, experts, and clients . . . in having better conversations with one another" and in helping "ameliorate structural and interpersonal factors which lead to alienation and domination" (538). Lisa Zanetti and Adrian Carr go somewhat further and argue for what they term "participatory research, . . . a blend of social activism and critical research methodology," which seeks "the development of self-reliant, self-assertive, and self-determinative communities" (1998, 367–368). This effort requires, in their view, that we explore "the psychological and political mechanisms that can be combined and utilized to overcome individual and collective resistance to social change" (358). Employing a somewhat opaque jargon often characteristic of this genre of writing, these theorists suggest that such an approach would serve to provide a "therapeutic setting" in which "both individual and collective catharsis takes place through the contextually-discovered revelation of, and reflection upon, the 'social amnesia' and resulting political quiescence that permit profoundly inegalitarian social conditions to remain in force" (1998, 358).

In other words, these writers argue that a therapeutic approach to political activism can help communities become psychologically better adjusted and, as a result, more willing to work for changes that will remedy the economic, political, and social ills that serve to oppress them. What is common to these critical theorists is that they all seem to see public administrators as serving somehow in a therapeutic role with members of the organization, clients, and others serving as their patients. These various "patients" in society are, in some real sense, "sick," and they need to be cured by public administrators of the psychological fixations, neuroses, obsessions, phobias, or delusions that blind them to the realities of their everyday existence. Richard Stillman, in my view, is correct, therefore, when he argues that these types of theorists often "seem to envision a sort of 'therapeutic state' with public administrators as 'the chief therapists'" (1995, 39). In doing so, although these authors often raise legitimate and important questions about the oppressive character of modern organizations and institutions, they end up, perhaps paradoxically, advocating much the same type of vision of the state as expressed in the mainstream literature, the major difference here being presumably that their "therapeutic state" would be led, or at least "counseled," by a more activist, egalitarian, socially aware, and enlightened brand of public administrator.

Conclusion

Despite many profound disagreements and conflicts in our field, many public administration writers have promoted then, whether consciously or not, the idea of the state as a purposive association and of government as a teleocracy. Classical writers, human relations authors, instrumental rationalists in public policy analysis and public management, reinventors, new public administrationists, and critical theorists often have radically different ideas about how to organize and manage public administration, about the role that politics and values should play in determining administrative actions, and about what is the appropriate character of scientific enquiry within public administration. Nonetheless, underlying much of this apparent diversity in approaches is an important unity in ideas about what a state is or should be. Waldo, in my view, is correct, therefore, when he argues that "the literature of public administration contains elements that are political theory as this is conventionally understood" (1984, x). Furthermore, my argument is lent specific support by Waldo's own observation that, despite their professed dedication to value-free scientific enquiry, public administration writers have often promoted a vision of a "Good Life" or "goals posited as the 'ends of the state'" (xxxvi). Waldo notes that this vision is nowadays expressed with a greater reticence than was true earlier in this century but insists, nonetheless, that it remains an ideal sought by writers.

There are important exceptions here. These include pluralist writers, such as Charles Lindblom (1959) and the late Aaron Wildavsky (1979), who, if they think about the state at all, see it largely in terms of an interplay of multiple and conflicting group purposes. Nonetheless, the vision of public administration as an instrument of a state organized around important substantive purposes clearly continues to exercise a strong hold over the minds of many major thinkers in our field. Of course, one might ask at this point why we should be so concerned about the dominance of this particular vision of the state in our literature. What does it matter that this vision is so strikingly similar to that expressed, for example, by Frederick the Great and the Prussian cameralist writers? So long as public administration writers are committed to principles of democracy and freedom, what do we, as Americans, have to fear from their vision of a purposive state? The purpose of the next two chapters is to seek to provide an answer to these important questions.

5
The Practical Limits of Teleocracy

In considering possible limitations of the view of public administration as an instrument in the service of a purposive state, it may be useful to begin by asking what it is that we would need in order to make the enactment of a vision of teleocratic governance and administration feasible or practical. The earlier discussion of the character of the vision of a purposive state indicates that, at a very minimum, two conditions must be met. First, political power must be sufficiently centralized within the structure of government so that the activities of its administrators can be directed toward the pursuit of a coherent set of substantive state purposes. As noted earlier, the availability of a powerful administrative apparatus is a key condition for the accomplishment of the ends of a purposive state. However, centralized political control over this administrative apparatus is also required if administrative power is to serve the ends of state. Of note in this regard is the fact that public administration writers, as we have seen, have often advocated strengthening the power of the chief executive over the activities of public administrators as a necessary condition for the promotion of what they see as effective and efficient government.

The second condition for successful teleocratic governance is that government leaders must possess a degree of knowledge sufficient to enable them to ascertain what particular policy actions they must undertake in order to promote the accomplishment of state ends. Such knowledge must include an awareness concerning just how individuals, groups, and organizations within society at large are likely to respond to government policies. Such knowledge becomes necessary in a purposive state because a teleocratic approach to governance requires not only that government be able to exercise power over the actions of its administrators but also that it be able to exercise power over the actions of its subjects. To accomplish the latter, it must possess knowledge as to how its policies affect the actions of its subjects.

In summary, therefore, the government of a purposive state must at the very least have sufficient power to direct the actions of its administrators so as to promote substantive state ends and, furthermore, sufficient knowledge about the effects of its policies on the actions of its subjects so that it can identify what those policies should be. There is good reason to believe, in fact, that neither of these conditions can be met within our existing system of political institutions, at least to the degree that would seem necessary for the running of a purposive state. This is because a vision of purposive association does not really describe the type of political association in which we live. It is only on rare occasions of national consensus, such as during World War II or the Great Depression, that our nation has really operated as anything close to a purposive association. Rather, for most of our history, our political practice has reflected a vision of the state as something more akin to a "civil association." This particular vision of the state was briefly discussed earlier. It will be useful now to explore this vision more fully so that we can understand better the practical limits that it places on a teleocratic approach to governance and administration.

The Vision of Civil Association

As noted earlier, a vision of the state as a civil association is one in which individuals recognize themselves as essentially free to pursue their own particular interests and their own particular values within the framework of a set of rules of conduct that limit the harm that they can do to each other. What binds the members of such an association together as a political entity is not the recognition of any set of common substantive ends or purposes. Rather, it is simply their acknowledgement that their actions should be conducted in such a manner that they conform to certain noninstrumental rules of conduct. As Michael Oakeshott observed, a civil association is one in which its members see themselves as "each pursuing his own interests or even joined with some others in seeking common satisfactions, but related to one another in the continuous acknowledgment of the authority of rules of conduct" (1975, 201). Civil association is, in Oakeshott's words, a "formal relationship in terms of rules" and "not a substantive relationship in terms of common action" (201). The purpose of such rules is not to secure the achievement of any particular set of substantive purposes. It is not to strive toward a more prosperous, a more healthy, a more godly, or a more equitable society. In fact, as Oakeshott argued, the rules of a civil association must be "indifferent to the success or to the failure of the substantive enterprises being pursued" by its members (1991, 454). The function of rules in a civil association can be only to define the parameters by which individuals and groups act and interact with each other as they pursue their own particular interests or purposes and, in doing so, to limit the harm that they can inflict on each other. A civil association can be seen here as akin to what Michael Polanyi, drawing on analogies from the physical sciences, has termed a system of "spontaneous order." Within such a social arrangement, according to Polanyi, "order is achieved among human beings by allowing them to interact with each other on their own initiative—subject only to laws which uniformly apply to all of them" (1998, 195).

Given a state constituted in this fashion, the role of government becomes largely that of elucidating, protecting, and enforcing the rules of conduct that govern individual and group actions and their interactions. As Oakeshott put it, within a civil association the concern of government, which can be termed a "nomocracy," is simply "to keep the conversation going, not to determine what is said" (1975, 202–203). This form of government is not designed or intended to promote the substantive interests or aspirations of any particular individual or group in society. Indeed, the rulers of a civil association, according to Oakeshott, should "have no substantive interest of their own," and they must be "indifferent to the substantive interests of their subjects" (1991, 455). The image of government in a civil association here is juridical rather than managerial. It is, as Oakeshott noted, "that of the umpire whose business it is to administer the rules of a game in which he does not himself participate" (1993, 49). Oakeshott observed that, in a civil association, "the office of government is not to impose other beliefs and activities upon its subjects, not to tutor or to educate them, not to make them better or happier in another way, not to direct them, to galvanize them into action, to lead them or to co-ordinate their activities so that no occasion of conflict shall occur" (1991, 427). Rather, the office of such a government is to "accept the current diversity of opinion and activity" and "to resolve some of the collisions which this variety of beliefs and activities generates; to preserve peace, not by placing an interdict upon choice and upon the diversity that springs from the exercise of preference, not by imposing substantive uniformity, but by enforcing general rules of procedure upon all subjects alike" (Oakeshott 1991, 427–428).

Writers on Civil Association

This vision of the state as a civil association and of government as a nomocracy is most clearly reflected in the writings of seventeenth- and eighteenth-century British philosophers. It is illustrated perhaps best in John Locke's argument, in his *Second Treatise of Government*, that "the great and chief end . . . of men's uniting into commonwealths, and putting themselves under government, is the preservation of their property," which Locke defines broadly as including "their lives, liberties, and estates" (1939, 453). According to Locke, "The great end of men's entering into society" is not a substantive end but rather is simply "the enjoyment of their properties in peace and safety" (457). "In Locke's scheme," as Thomas Pangle argues, "there is no basis for supposing that human nature requires or inclines toward a government that defines for its subjects their happiness, virtue, or salvation" (Pangle 1990, 72). Furthermore, government, in Locke's view, is not free to pursue whatever ends or purposes that it chooses but is itself subject to rules of conduct. As Locke argued forcefully, government cannot "possibly be absolutely arbitrary over the lives and fortunes of the people" (Locke 1939, 457). Rather, government "is bound to dispense justice, and decide the rights of the subject by promulgated standing laws, and known authorized judges" (458). From Locke's perspective, within what he terms a "political or civil society" (433), the community "comes to be umpire; and by understanding indifferent rules and men authorized by the community for their execution, decides all the differences that may happen between any members of that society concerning any matter of right, and punishes those offenses . . . against the society with such penalties as the law has established" (437).

Locke emphasized that the laws in such a "civil society" are to be administered not only in an impartial but also in a predictable fashion. What is required of government by men and women is "an established, settled, known law" (1939, 454). As Locke argued in what is perhaps his clearest summary of the ideal character of civil association, "freedom of men under government is to have a standing rule to live by, common to everyone of that society, and made by the legislative power erected in it; a liberty to follow my own will in all things, where that rule prescribes not; and not to be subject to the inconstant, uncertain, unknown, arbitrary will of another man" (412).

What Locke presents here, therefore, is a powerful vision of civil association and nomocratic governance. David Hume expressed a similar vision. According to Hume, man is "engaged to establish political society, in order to establish justice; without which there can be no peace among them, nor safety, nor mutual intercourse" (1987, 37). The "vast apparatus of our government" has, for Hume, "ultimately no other object or purpose but the distribution of justice" (37). This justice, according to Hume, cannot be directed at seeking any particular substantive outcomes for the community. It can consist only of the impartial application of laws. Hume argued here that the "avidity and partiality of men wou'd quickly bring disorder into the world, if not restrain'd by some general and inflexible principles" and that, as a result, "men have establish'd those principles, and have agreed to restrain themselves by general rules, which are unchangeable by spite and favour, and by particular views of private or public interest" (1984, 584). Hume saw the impartial application of general laws as essential to limiting the power of government over its citizens, arguing that a government that "receives the appellation of free . . . must act by general and equal laws" (1987, 40–41).

Finally, Edmund Burke made clear his own particular vision of civil association when, in criticizing the French Revolution, he argued that true liberty is "*social* freedom . . . that state of affairs in which liberty is secured by the equality of restraint" and "in which the liberty of no one man, and no body of men, and no number of men, can find means to trespass on the liberty of any person, or any description of persons, in the society" (1992, 7–8). This "kind of liberty," according to Burke, "is but another name for justice" (8). It is one in which the citizen "is in a perfect state of legal security, with regard to his life, to his property, to the uncontrolled disposal of his person, to the free use of his industry and his faculties" (8).

Consistent with his vision of civil association, Burke saw the role of government primarily as constraining the exercise of human passions. According to Burke, "Government is a contrivance of human wisdom to provide for human *wants*," and "among these wants is to be reckoned the want" of individuals "of a sufficient restraint upon their passions" (1955, 68). "The great use of government," Burke argued, "is as a restraint" (1999, 195). This meant for Burke that citizens, whether in the private sphere or public sphere, should be limited in the pursuit of their own purposes by a system of laws indifferent to those purposes. As Burke noted, "Even in the mass and body, as well as in the individuals, the inclinations of men should frequently be thwarted, their will controlled, and their passions brought into subjection," which "can only be done *by a power out of themselves*," and not "subject to that will and to those passions which is its office to bridle and subdue" (1955, 68–69).

The Practice of Civil Association

I observed earlier that our ideas about the state do not emerge in a vacuum but are generally a result of reflections on the practices of existing governments. This observation is as true of the vision of civil association as it is true of the vision of purposive association. At least three aspects of European and especially English political practice are worth mentioning here. First, the Middle Ages saw a significant, albeit an incomplete, extension of monarchical control over the judicial systems of their territories. As a result, by the fifteenth century the idea of governance as a juridical activity had become widely accepted among the subjects of the monarch. As Oakeshott has argued, "The realm was on the way to becoming a 'sovereign' civil association and the ruler's *majestas* was that of a judge" (1975, 213). Noteworthy in this regard is the fact that the English Parliament of the thirteenth and fourteenth centuries was seen primarily as a court of law. Oakeshott notes that Parliament was "set over other courts for resolving difficult or doubtful judgements and providing new remedies for newly emergent wrongs and meting out justice to all according to their deserts" (1996, 77–78).

Second, again beginning in the Middle Ages, there occurred a gradual, admittedly intermittent, but nonetheless perceptible weakening of the power of feudal institutions. This situation stemmed partly from the aforementioned attempts of monarchs to assert their power over their domains. One important by-product of this weakening of feudal power was that many of the monarch's subjects became increasingly able to exert more power over their own lives. They began to think of themselves more as free individuals than as members of a feudal organism or community. Starting as early as the thirteenth century, as Oakeshott argued, "extended opportunities of escape from the cor-

porate and communal organizations of current medieval life offered
themselves . . . in varying degrees all over the continent of Europe, not
in towns only . . . but even in the countryside. And all that had hitherto
been governed by immemorial custom and had derived from status in a
community—occupations, duties, beliefs, responsibilities—was beginning to respond to the choices of individuals" (1993, 21).

This emerging sense of individuality was motivated not by abstract
ideas of political association but by the practical choices made by men
and not infrequently also by women in response to their own particular day-to-day problems and the opportunities created by the weakening of feudal and communal ties. As Oakeshott noted, these changes
"were not shaped by men inspired by a comprehensive new way of
living" but rather "were explored (often hesitatingly) by those who saw,
perhaps in one of them, an occasion which seemed to meet an immedi-
ate need" (1993, 21). Notwithstanding the practical roots of this idea,
by the sixteenth century, there began to emerge what Oakeshott termed
a "morality of individuality," a "disposition to make choices for oneself
. . . concerning activities, occupations, beliefs, opinions, duties, and
responsibilities" and a disposition "to approve of this sort of conduct
. . . as conduct proper to a human being" (20–21).

Finally, starting in the late fifteenth century, the increasing power of
monarchs over the lives of their subjects, which, as we have seen, the
development of an administrative apparatus had made possible, began
to lead perhaps not surprisingly to what were seen by some of their
subjects as abuses of that power. These perceived abuses of power
prompted attempts by groups of citizens to circumscribe or to place
limits on the exercise of expanding monarchical power. In this process,
the opponents of monarchical power often made use of some of the
same institutions that monarchs had used earlier to help assert their
own authority over their territories, including royal courts and parlia-
ments as well as older feudal institutions such as common law courts.
The growing sense of individuality among the population, mentioned
above, was also important here in that it not only fueled a demand for
a powerful government that could break down feudal ties and privi-
leges but also contributed to an appropriate suspicion or uneasiness
about the growing power of the European monarchs. In doing so, it
motivated a desire to place limits on their power. This increasing disposition to try to place limits on expanding monarchical power is seen

most clearly in the long struggle between the king and his Parliament in seventeenth-century England, a struggle that resulted first in the bloody English Civil War and then some forty years or so later in the bloodless coup termed by its instigators the "Glorious Revolution." I admit that the causes of these conflicts were complex and that a significant part of the desire to limit monarchical power may well have been motivated not by any particular vision of the state but simply by the selfish desires of many landowners, merchants, tradesmen, and professionals seeking to protect their own economic interests against increasing monarchical encroachment. Nonetheless, out of such historical practices the idea of the state as a civil association began to take on a much clearer form. Indeed, it was the experience of seventeenth-century England that was particularly important in providing Locke with much of the inspiration for his political thinking. As Oakeshott argued, Locke's *Second Treatise* should not be read as "a preface to political activity" but rather as a "postscript" (1991, 53). It is "a brief conspectus of the manner in which Englishmen were accustomed to go about the business of attending to their arrangements—a brilliant abridgment of the political habits of Englishmen" (53).

Civil Association and the Constitution

This vision of the state as a civil association is, of course, essentially the same one that has been handed down to us through the centuries as part of our own Anglo-American tradition of political practice. It is a vision shaped in considerable part by reflections such as those of Locke on the struggle between Parliament and the Stuart monarchs in seventeenth-century England, and it is a vision that continues to shape our political, economic, and social order. A civil association, as Oakeshott has argued, forms the type of state that "was assumed . . . by the authors of the Federalist papers (particularly James Madison), and by the framers of the Constitution" (1975, 244). It is true that the Constitution, of course, lays out certain objectives, namely, "to form a more perfect Union, establish Justice, insure domestic Tranquillity, provide for the common Defense, promote the general Welfare, and secure the blessings of Liberty" (Wills 1982, 452). These objectives, however, would seem concerned predominantly with the establishment of rules and conditions for a civil association within which individuals, on their own or in concert with others, can peacefully pursue their interests or visions of the public good. They do not seem to constitute the substantive ends of a purposive association.

Indeed, Madison's vision of civil association is openly revealed in his assertion that "the first object of government" is the protection of "diversity in the faculties of men" (Wills 1982, 43–44). Madison makes it clear here that he is talking about "the protection of different and unequal faculties of acquiring property" (44). Such protection is necessary because "government is instituted no less for protection of the property, than of the persons of individuals" (278). Consistent with this Lockean vision of limited government, Madison saw the "principal task of modern Legislation" as the regulation of the "various and interfering interests" of individuals in the community (44). For Madison, it is justice that is the "end of government" and "the end of civil society" (265). Such justice cannot exist in a society, in Madison's view, "where the stronger faction can readily unite and oppress the weaker" anymore than it can exist "where the weaker individual is not secured against the violence of the stronger" (265). Furthermore, Madison's writings reveal clearly his reservations about any idea of the state as a purposive association. Madison argued that it was "impracticable" to assume that every citizen would have "the same opinions, the same passions, and the same interests" and that "the diversity in the faculties of men" was "an insuperable object to a uniformity of interests" (Wills 1982, 43–44). Consequently, he thought humankind "much more disposed to vex and oppress each other, than to cooperate for their common good" (44).

Because of his awareness of the dangers to liberty posed by these conflicting interests and passions, Madison deliberately sought, by the use of constitutional checks on power, to render more difficult the achievement of substantive common purposes through government by any particular group in the community. For example, Madison argued for the Union because he believed that a stronger central government would help check the ability of majority factions in state legislatures to achieve their own substantive ends at the expense of minorities. He argued that "if a majority be united by a common interest, the rights of the minority will be insecure" (Wills 1982, 264). The "security for civil rights," for Madison, consists "in the multiplicity of interests" (264). He noted, "Extend the sphere, and you take in a greater variety of parties and interests; you make it less probable that a majority of the whole will have a common motive to invade the rights of other citizens; or if such a common motive exists, it will be more difficult for all who feel it to discover their own strength, and to act in unison with each other" (Wills 1982, 48). In this way, Madison sought consciously to frustrate the achievement of any particular set of substantive ends by majorities in state legislatures. At the same time, Madison also argued for a separation of powers as a means of limiting the ability of majorities at the federal level to achieve their substantive ends. A separation of powers between the legislative, executive, and judicial branches of government was necessary because "ambition must be made to counteract ambition" (Wills 1982, 262) and to overcome "the defect of better motives" by providing for "opposite and rival interests" (263).

Alexander Hamilton revealed a similar view of the state when he wrote that a strong executive was essential in domestic matters to "the steady administration of the laws, to the protection of property against those irregular and high handed combinations, which sometimes interrupt the ordinary course of justice" and to "the security of liberty against the enterprise and assaults of ambition, of faction and of anarchy" (Wills 1982, 355). In other words, the virtue of a strong executive, for Hamilton, lay in significant part in its role as a check on the ability of legislative majorities to achieve their substantive ends. Similarly, for Hamilton, the courts were to serve as "bulwarks . . . against legislative encroachments" and to protect "the constitution and the rights of individuals" from "the effects of occasional ill humours in the society" (397). Hamilton saw the principal domestic task of government as limiting the harm that individuals and groups could inflict on each other. As he saw it, government was "instituted" because "the passions of men will not conform to the dictates of reason and justice, without constraint" (72).

The founders' Constitution, with its various devices for checking power, can be seen here, therefore, as providing agreed-on rules of association for individuals and groups as they seek to achieve their own interests or particularistic visions of the public good within the political process. The effect of these constitutional rules is to place boundaries on the conduct of individuals and groups within the process of policy formulation and implementation and, in doing so, to limit the power that particular individuals and groups can exert over others. As such, the founders' Constitution can be seen as an essential part of the larger set of rules of a civil association.

In asserting the importance of the idea of civil association in the political vision of the founders, I do not mean to suggest that the vision of a purposive state has had no influence at all on American political and constitutional history. Indeed, as Oakeshott (1975) himself argued, the discourse and practice of all real-world modern states inevitably reflect a tension between the two visions of civil and purposive association. My point here is simply that the American state and its form of limited government reflect in large part a vision of civil association.

The Constitution, Power, and Public Administration

The fact that our Constitution has its roots largely in a Lockean vision of civil association has important implications for the exercise of political power within our system of government. In particular, it means that political power is not concentrated in any one branch or, for that matter, any one level of government. Instead of there being a single locus of power, power is fragmented. It is dispersed throughout our constitutional system. Each of the multiple checks on the exercise of power within the system becomes itself an independent source of political power, and each source of such power is in turn checked by the others. Richard Stillman puts this best perhaps when he notes that power in our Constitution is "continuously being smashed and in perpetual motion; unstoppable, moving, hard to locate" (1990, 165). It is "always up for grabs: vague, imprecise, hard to pin down, free to shift anytime and everywhere" (165). This fragmentation of political power has the effect of limiting the ability of any particular group of political leaders to impose their political objectives on others in the political process. As a result, except in rare times of national crisis, our constitutional system of government does not and cannot act as a vehicle for the articulation of any coherent set of national purposes. It becomes instead a means for seeking agreements on action between individuals and groups with separate and often conflicting private and public purposes. Within this type of civil association, legislation typically reflects not a common set of purposes but simply a compromise between the different and conflicting purposes of different legislative factions.

The fact that our political process does not as a rule provide a means of voicing a coherent set of purposes has important implications for public administration. It renders somewhat impractical, if not downright absurd, any notion that public administration might serve in general as a unified instrument by which the state could achieve any coherent set of substantive purposes. Within a system of governance in which the power of any one group of leaders can be always checked by another, there is simply no one institution—not the president, nor the Congress, nor the bureaucracy itself, for that matter— that has the power to direct public administrators to do this. No one leader or group of leaders, even if they were able and willing to formulate a plan of action for the achievement of a coherent set of national ends, would have sufficient power over the apparatus of administration to be able to implement these ends.

Contemporary writings on the American administrative state provide ample evidence of the limits of the power of political leaders over the activities of administrators (Meier 1979; Wilson 1989). It was Norton Long, however, who some half a century ago saw most clearly perhaps the constraints that our constitutional system of governance placed on our ability to pursue a teleocratic style of governance and administration. In critiquing the orthodox view of public administration as a neutral instrument of the will of political leaders, Long observed that, in our system, "power is not concentrated by the structure of government or politics into the hands of a leadership with a capacity to budget it among a diverse set of administrative agencies" (1949, 258). According to Long, public administrators simply "cannot depend on the formal chain of command to deliver them enough political power to permit them to do their jobs" (258). As a result, public administrators must seek political power to support their actions from a diverse set of political leaders and client groups, and their activities become subject to the scrutiny, power, and influence of a multitude of different political actors, each with their own particular agendas. Public administrators find themselves, according to Long, working within "a structure of interests friendly or hostile, vague and general or compact and well-defined" so that power flows "in from the sides of an organization" and also "up the organization to the center from the constituent parts" (258).

Many public administration writers have, as noted earlier, focused their hopes for a teleocratic system of governance and administration on a strong and enlightened presidency. Long, however, recognized specifically just how inadequate was the power of the president as chief executive in our constitutional system to direct administrative agencies and how this lack of power impeded teleocratic governance and administration. According to Long, "The broad alliance of conflicting groups that makes up presidential majorities scarcely coheres about any pattern of objectives nor has it . . . had its collective power concentrated in an accepted leadership with a personal mandate" (1949, 259). Long argued that the "integration of the administrative structure through an over-all purpose in terms of which tasks and priorities can be established is an emergency phenomenon" (260). He noted that it is "only in crises," such as war or depression, that "the powers of the Executive" are "nearly adequate to impose a common plan of action on the executive branch" and that "in ordinary times the manifold pressures of our pluralistic society work themselves out in accordance with the balance of forces prevailing in Congress and the agencies" (260). Under normal conditions, in Long's view, "the program of the President cannot be a Gosplan for the government precisely because the nature of his institutional and group support gives him insufficient power" (260).

Long clearly believed, then, that our political system simply lacked a sufficient concentration of political power to provide administrators with any coherent plan or set of substantive objectives that they would be obliged to follow. He ridiculed as a "will-o'-the wisp" the assumption made by his fellow public administration writers that "there must be something akin to Rousseau's *volonté générale* in administration to which the errant *volonté de tous* of the bureaus can and should be made to conform" (Long 1949, 260). The practical implementation of a political system driven by a single coherent will or set of purposes requires, in Long's view, "at least the potency of the British Labour Party and elsewhere has needed the disciplined organization of a fascist, nazi, or communist party to provide the power and consensus necessary to coordinate the manifold activities of government to a common plan" (261). Given the decentralized character of political power in our own system, he saw as improbable the notion of "a government integrated about a paramount national purpose" (263).

This fragmentation of political power explains the difficulties that successive presidents since Franklin Roosevelt have experienced in attempting to use administrative reform as a device to strengthen their power over the activities of federal agencies at the expense of Congress. The executive and legislative branches of government, each accorded a share of political power by the founders under the Constitution, have been unwilling to cede power over public administration to the other. In the struggle between the president and the Congress for control of the bureaucracy, as James Q. Wilson has argued, "every advance in the power of the president [over the bureaucracy] has been matched by a comparable advance in Congress" (1989, 259). The inevitable result has been that, despite repeated attempts by each branch of government to gain control over the apparatus of administration, public administrators have remained answerable to different masters. They are not simply an instrument to be used at will by a particular group of political leaders.

Our constitution, therefore, because it reflects so strongly a vision of civil association, makes it difficult for any one leader or group of leaders to use public administration as an instrument by which they might consistently carry out a coherent set of substantive state ends. As such, our Constitution represents a significant practical impediment for those who would seek a more unified, a more rational, and a more teleocratic form of governance and administration. Still, it is not simply the fragmentation of political power over public administration that makes difficult the attainment of a teleocratic form of governance and administration. Also important are the limits that our form of civil association places on the power that government officials, including public administrators, can exercise over the actions of citizens. In order to see these limits on governmental power, we need to understand the nature of the constraints that a civil association places on the knowledge that government officials can have regarding the actions of citizens in society.

Civil Association and Social Science

An important implication of having a state that strongly reflects a vision of civil association is that, when compared to a purposive state, civil association allows individuals and groups in society to exercise a substantially greater degree of discretion or freedom in regard to their actions. In a purposive association, individual actions must be made conducive to the attainment of the substantive ends of the state. Individuals, either out of a sense of commitment to the ends of the state or out of fear of punishment by government, must conform their actions to the ends of the purposive association. The range of their possible actions is, therefore, significantly circumscribed. On the other hand, in a civil association it is not necessary that individuals undertake particular actions that conform to certain substantive ends of the state because a civil association does not explicitly posit any such ends. Individuals in a civil association are permitted substantial discretion over their actions within a framework of rules that serves to limit the harm that their actions can impose on others. Although these rules prohibit certain types of actions, they typically do not mandate any particular actions so that the scope of possible actions available to individuals, whether acting alone or within groups, is considerably greater than the range that prevails under a purposive association.

The fact that individuals and groups are permitted to exercise substantial discretion in choosing their actions within a civil association in turn has important implications for social science. This discretion affects the scope and nature of the knowledge that they use in deciding on such actions. In particular, given the availability of individual discretion over their own actions within a civil association, much of the information or knowledge that men and women use in deciding on what actions they will undertake is inevitably dispersed. Such information is, therefore, inaccessible to any single mind or group of minds, including those of social scientists. As Friedrich Hayek (1948, 1973) argued, much of the knowledge used in undertaking actions within this type of social order (one that, following Polanyi, he termed a "spontaneous order") comes into existence only as individuals seek to discover facts that may be to their advantage in particular situations. In other words, such knowledge is not given. It can only be discovered as individuals work on the particular tasks that they themselves have chosen to undertake. It is an ordinary or practical type of knowledge often based on experience and practice rather than on scientific analysis. It is, as Hayek observed, a "knowledge of people, of local conditions, and of special circumstances" (1948, 80). Hayek illustrated both the character and the importance of such knowledge in an economic context when he argued that

> to know of and to put to use a machine not fully employed, or somebody's skill which could be better utilized, or to be aware of a surplus stock which can be

drawn upon during an interruption of supplies, is socially quite as useful as a knowledge of better alternative techniques. The shipper who earns his living from using otherwise empty or half-filled journeys of tramp-steamers, or the estate agent whose whole knowledge is almost exclusively one of temporary opportunities, or the *arbitrageur* who gains from local differences of commodity prices—are all performing eminently useful functions based on special knowledge of circumstances of the fleeting moment not known to others (80).

The usefulness of such practical knowledge must always lie in the context of the particular time and place in which it is acquired. As a result, different knowledge may become relevant in different times and different places. Being specific to time and place, this knowledge cannot be readily at the command of everybody. Rather, it is acquired by those of us who find it useful in our particular jobs or tasks in society. Furthermore, much of this knowledge does not even consist of facts as such, at least not facts as social scientists would understand them. It consists rather of opinions about facts. It is often an essentially subjective form of knowledge in that it reflects the different views of reality that we as individuals bring to bear as we make choices about our actions. In light of this situation, it becomes even more apparent that much of the knowledge that individuals use in deciding on their actions in a civil association is inaccessible to a single mind or group of minds. In Hayek's words, such subjective knowledge cannot exist "as an integrated whole or in one mind" but rather consists of "the separate and often inconsistent and even conflicting views of different people" (1979, 92).

The scope and nature of the knowledge used by individuals within a civil association suggest inherent limits on the type of knowledge that social science can provide for public administration and public policy. The social scientist who seeks to make predictions about the effects of public policies on the interrelated actions of individuals in particular situations must do so in the absence of much, if not most, of the knowledge that those individuals themselves use in deciding their actions in those situations. As Hayek noted, in the social sciences "individual events regularly depend on so many concrete circumstances that we shall never in fact be in a position to ascertain them all," and, consequently, "the ideal of prediction and control must largely remain beyond our reach" (1967, 34).

This limitation on our knowledge is illustrated in economics, where theorists frequently develop highly elegant mathematical models that explain the operation of particular markets but that contain variables that we cannot possibly observe. These models may help us understand how such markets work. They may even enable us to make predictions about the general kinds of outcomes we might expect or might not expect from certain kinds of events or government policies. They cannot, however, as a rule, provide us with predictions about the specific effects of a given policy in a particular situation. Anyone who doubts this must explain why it is that economists are not all millionaires (McCloskey 1990). As a result, therefore, although we as social scientists may sometimes be able to understand the principles that govern certain human actions, to predict the kinds of actions that might occur as a result of particular government policies assuming certain conditions, and even sometimes to exclude the possibility of certain actions, we will often find it impossible to foresee the specific effects of such policies in particular situations. As Hayek noted with respect to economics, we are "confined to describing kinds of patterns which will appear if certain general conditions are satisfied, but can rarely if ever derive from this knowledge any predictions of specific phenomena" (1967, 35). Frank Ward, an economist from the University of Tennessee in the 1940s, perhaps captured this idea more colorfully when he told his students that "the study of economics won't keep you out of the breadline: but at least you'll know why you're there" (Buchanan 1979, 37).

Therefore, despite the accomplishments of social science, government officials seeking to make decisions will always face considerable, if not overwhelming, uncertainty regarding the consequences of alternative policy interventions within a civil association. As Hayek warned, "The more indirect and remote effects" of policy interventions "will mostly be unknown" (1973, 57), and "many well-intentioned measures may have a long train of unforeseeable and undesirable consequences" (59). What we must recognize within a civil association is what Hayek terms "the necessary and irremediable ignorance on everyone's part of most of the particular facts which determine the actions of all the several members of human society" (1973, 12).

The foregoing may help explain the frankly disappointing record of the social sciences as a tool for policy making and public administration. Given the high degree of unpredictability of human action within our civil association, we should not be surprised that the social sciences have not been able, as Terence Mitchell and William Scott put it, to produce "anything approximating law-like generalizations which would apply to such major issues as policy formulation, decision making, and strategy" (1987, 447). Neither should we be surprised when Charles Lindblom observes that there is an "absence of undeniable evidence" in the social sciences and that it is difficult to "identify a single social science finding or idea that is undeniably indispensable to any social task or effort" (1990, 136).

Significant constraints on the predictive power of social science within our civil association exist, therefore, because such an association allows individuals to exercise a substantial degree of discretion in their actions and thereby to draw on knowledge that is inaccessible to social scientists. The economist Frank Knight saw this when he argued that if we accept that man "is a free or problem-solving entity or being, . . . his doings as behavior events are ultimately more or less indeterminate, and cannot even theoretically be exhaustively predicted or described in advance" (1982, 278). According to Knight, the "fact of freedom is connected with and accounts for the peculiar heterogeneity and unpredictable variability in time . . . as factual characteristics of human phenomena" (279).

Civil association, in increasing the unpredictability of human actions, therefore, inevitably sets limits on the knowledge that social science can provide to government about the effects of its policies on the actions of its subjects. In doing so, civil association severely inhibits the ability of government to engage in a teleocratic style of governance and administration. We could no doubt significantly reduce, although certainly not eliminate, this unpredictability were we prepared to reorganize ourselves as a state along the lines of purposive association. Under purposive political association, our actions would become more predictable because they would be governed by the ends of the state. The obvious fact that most of us would be uncomfortable with the prospect of living in such a state, however, is itself evidence of the not inconsiderable power of the vision of civil association in shaping the type of state in which we have become accustomed to living.

Conclusion

In summary, therefore, we have inherited traditions or habits of political practice, as revealed in our Constitution, that reflect a vision of the state that is much closer to the idea of a civil association than that of a purposive association. Notwithstanding the aspirations of many public administration writers, this tradition places significant limits on our capacity to pursue a teleocratic form of governance and administration. Given our tradition of constitutionally limited government, our government leaders are generally not able to exercise the type of power over the administrative apparatus that would render it a suitable instrument for the achievement of a coherent set of substantive state purposes. Furthermore, given the relative freedom of action available to citizens within our civil association, neither they nor their public administrators nor their statisticians possess the kind of knowledge of the effects of government actions on society that would be necessary to make government an instrument for the effective accomplishment of such purposes. In other words, our inherited habits and institutions of civil association, to a considerable degree, rob us of both the concentrated power and the knowledge that we would need to carry out effectively the enactment of a vision of teleocratic governance and administration.

6

Postmodernity and the State

As the last chapter made clear, as inheritors of a particular set of political and constitutional traditions, we are inevitably to some degree constrained by the pressures of the past in our ability to adopt a more teleocratic style of governance and administration. We are also, however, constrained by the pressures of the present and at least the foreseeable future. In particular, as I shall argue in this chapter, the pursuit of a vision of a purposive state, governed and managed by a teleocracy, may be not only impractical but also potentially harmful in light of the severe fragmentation of political culture that is characteristic of what many observers have termed the postmodern condition. I will further suggest here that the idea of civil association, which we explored in the previous chapter, may well provide a vision of the state that is much more in keeping with the character of our fragmented postmodern political culture.

The Postmodern Condition

The postmodern condition and its implications for public administration have become a topic of increasing interest among public administration writers (Fox and Miller 1995; Farmer 1995, 1998; McSwite 1997). Central to postmodern thinking is the idea that there has been a decline in the credibility or in the legitimating power of the grand narratives or stories that we are used to telling each other about both politics and science in society. The postmodern condition is one of what the French postmodernist philosopher Jean-François Lyotard has termed an "incredulity toward metanarratives" (1984, xxiv). Such metanarratives include, according to Lyotard, "the progressive emancipation of reason and freedom, the progressive or catastrophic emancipation of labor, . . . the enrichment of all humanity through the progress of capitalist technoscience, and even . . . the salvation of creatures through the conversion of souls to the Christian narrative of martyred love" (1993, 17–18).

In other words, in the postmodern condition we no longer believe that we can root our political thinking and actions in the soil of the various versions of Enlightenment dogma, be they conservative, liberal, or socialistic. The grand stories that paint a picture of society moving forward, either in an incremental or in a revolutionary fashion, in the direction of some sort of scientific, economic, communitarian, or, for that matter, spiritual utopia no longer ring quite true. The defining political characteristic of the condition in which we find ourselves is not that of any particular grand metanarrative but rather that of a variety or of a plurality of local and often conflicting political narratives or stories. The stories that we tell ourselves about life and about politics are becoming increasingly particularistic and also increasingly heterogeneous. As Agnes Heller and Ferenc Fehér have observed, "The postmodern political condition is premissed on the acceptance of the plurality of cultures and discourses. Pluralism (of various kinds) is implicit in postmodernity as a project. The breakdown of the grand narrative is a direct invitation to cohabitation amongst various (local, cultural, ethnic, religious, 'ideological') small narratives" (1988, 5).

What defines the postmodern condition is a diversity in place of a uniformity: a diversity of values, a diversity of cultures, a diversity of traditions, and a diversity of styles of life. John Gray, a contemporary British political philosopher, captures this idea of postmodernist diversity vividly when he observes that today

> almost all of us live in societies which are not unified by any single cultural tradition, but which contain a variety of traditions and ways of life. Our great cities shelter vast enclaves of traditional life, often introduced by recent immigrants, at the same time as they nurture liberal bohemian milieux where conduct is governed by taste and preference rather than by any set of established mores. . . . Our societies encompass a kaleidoscopic diversity of attitudes to sexuality and gender, death and the human condition, even as they harbour a prodigious diversity of ethnic inheritances and styles of life (1993, 253).

Our condition is one in which, as Gray argues, "society intimates a diversity of possibly incommensurable values and world-views" (1993, 253). This postmodern political condition reveals itself concretely in a variety of ways. It is seen, at the global level, in the collapse of the Soviet Union and in the worldwide reassertion of ethnic, racial, religious, and tribal loyalties and conflicts, sometimes violent. It appears in the United States in the emergence of various forms of identity politics based on race, gender, disability, sexual preference, and lifestyle and in pressures for multicultural perspectives in school and university curricula. It is also evidenced in the increasing visibility and power of various religious groups in politics and in the increasing polarization of political discourse between political parties.

Following the jargon of postmodernist writers, we can think about the postmodern condition in terms of a multiplicity of language games, that is to say, systems of communication (Wittgenstein 1960). A language game can be seen here as somewhat like a game of chess or a game of cards. It is a game with its own particular set of rules: in this case, rules for engagement in a particular kind of conversation or discourse. A language game determines the kinds of utterances that are considered appropriate or, for that matter, inappropriate to a given kind of conversation. In other words, it affects what can be said and what cannot be said. A language game is, as Lyotard observes, a set of statements in which "the statements are 'moves' made by the players within the framework of generally applicable rules; these rules are specific to each particular kind of knowledge, and the 'moves' judged to be 'good' in one cannot be of the same type as those judged 'good' in another" (1984, 26). What happens in the postmodern condition is the emergence of a multiplicity of heterogeneous and incommensurable language games or what Lyotard terms an "'atomization' of the social into flexible networks of language games" (17). Each of these various language games contains its own ideas about what is "good" or what is "true," and there is no overarching accepted language game or metalanguage available to us that might resolve the conflicts between them.

The postmodern condition consists, therefore, in an extreme pluralism of often conflicting notions about what is "good" or what is "true." As such, the postmodern condition forces us to confront what Isaiah Berlin believed always to be true, namely, that "values can clash" and that "they can be incompatible between cultures, or groups in the same culture, or between you and me" (1992, 12). It forces us to acknowledge the possibility of pluralism, the possibility, to use Berlin's words, "that there might exist ends . . . equally ultimate, but incompatible with one another, that there might exist no single universal overarching standard that would enable a man to choose rationally between them" (1982, 69). The postmodern condition renders incredible any type of monist idea of a "unity or harmony of human ends," any idea that "all truly good things are linked to one another in single, perfect whole; or, at the very least, cannot be incompatible with one another" (Berlin 1969, x).

Postmodern Cultural Conflict

In light of the above, one does not need necessarily to penetrate the sometimes opaque jargon of postmodernist writers or to embrace postmodern thinking itself in order to recognize that the postmodern condition of cultural fragmentation is always, potentially at least, one of a high degree of cultural conflict. When we have a plurality of incommensurable narratives, a diversity of language games and values, and there is no overarching standard or measuring rod by which to settle incompatibilities or disputes among them, conflict can be expected to become the norm rather than the exception. James Davison Hunter (1990, 1994) has provided a vivid picture of what is at least one important aspect of this postmodern cultural conflict in the American context in his colorful account of what he terms "culture wars." Hunter documents here the deep, bitter, and often seemingly irresolvable and interminable ideological conflicts in American society that seem to occur between different cultural groups on a host of social issues. Such issues are very familiar to us. They include those of abortion, gay rights, immigration, euthanasia, affirmative action, AIDS policy, educational curricula and textbooks, sexually explicit art, school prayer, sexual harassment, and so on. For Hunter, there is far more to contemporary disputes over these types of issues than just a simple "political squabble" between political liberals and conservatives (1990, 118). Nor can the character of such disputes be explained in terms of class conflict because the lines of conflict so frequently cut across the lines of class. Rather, what Hunter sees is a "political and social hostility rooted in different systems of moral understanding," rooted in different bases "by which people determine whether something is good or bad, right or wrong, acceptable or unacceptable, and so on" (42). It is a conflict he sees as revolving "around our most fundamental and cherished assumptions about how to order our lives—our own lives and our lives together in this society" (42). What is going on out there, in a myriad of cultural disputes, is, according to Hunter, no less than a "fairly comprehensive and momentous struggle to define the meaning of America—

of how and on what terms will Americans live together, of what comprises the good society" (51).

Hunter's writings make clear the essentially postmodern character of this cultural conflict. He observes how contesting progressive and orthodox groups, in arguing about political issues, do not even "operate on the same plane of moral discussion" (Hunter 1990, 118) and how each side "speaks with a different moral vocabulary" (128). Whereas orthodox groups remain committed to a "transcendent foundation for moral judgement," progressivist forces reject such a foundation and believe that religious faiths and traditions must be continuously reinterpreted, continuously reinvented in light of "new circumstances and conditions" and "new challenges and needs" (122–123). The culture war is a struggle, then, according to Hunter, between "two distinct conceptions of moral authority—two different ways of apprehending reality, of ordering experience, of making moral judgements" (128). It is "a struggle to achieve or maintain the power to define reality" (52). In such a struggle, contending groups have little or no hope of trying to persuade each other of the merits of their respective positions or of reaching any type of compromise by engaging in a process of argumentation. Dialogue and compromise have become largely irrelevant because, as Hunter observes, "in the final analysis, each side of the cultural divide can only talk past the other" (131).

Hunter's thesis that we are in the midst of a war between incommensurable cultures is lent support by Gertrude Himmelfarb's writings. Borrowing from Disraeli's well-known metaphor, Himmelfarb (1998) suggests that we have become "two nations," divided along the lines of ethos and culture. She writes of the "moral polarization of society" that is conspicuous on such "hotly disputed issues as school vouchers, prayer in public schools, partial-birth abortions, pornography on the Internet, or homosexuality and adultery in the military," but she also suggests that the ramifications of this moral conflict are much broader and affect attitudes and beliefs on a "host of subjects ranging from private morality to public policy" (Himmelfarb 1998, 14). Indeed, Himmelfarb goes as far as to suggest that our moral polarization is "more profoundly divisive than the class polarization that Marxists looked to as a precondition for their revolution" (14–15).

Himmelfarb's reference to "revolution" here would seem ominous and would appear to raise the possibility of outbreaks of violence in the postmodern political clash of cultures. Hunter makes it clear that he himself uses the term "culture war" as a metaphor in his writings for the cultural differences that divide us within our culture. It is worth noting, however, that he also is not willing to dismiss entirely the possibility of even violent conflict between contesting cultural groups. Indeed, Hunter draws some disturbing parallels between our own cultural divisions and the civil strife that has occurred in such areas of the world as Yugoslavia, Ireland, and Lebanon. He notes that

> here, as there, nonnegotiable claims about the ordering of public life are in conflict. Here, as there, the claims made (even if thought of as secular) are religious in character, if not in substance—they emerge out of our ultimate beliefs and commitments, our most cherished sense of what is right, true, and good. Here, as there, the conflicting claims trace quickly back to competing ideals of community and national identity. Finally here, as there, a culture war with deep historical roots has festered just barely beneath the surface of public life (Hunter 1994, 227).

Lest Hunter's warning be thought of as simply alarmist or sensationalist, we might call to mind the bombing of a federal building in Oklahoma, the violence of Ruby Ridge and Waco, the arrest of a gunman in the halls of Congress, the bombing of abortion clinics, and the shooting of obstetricians who perform abortions. Recent events provide more than ample evidence of the potentially dangerous, the almost Hobbesian nature, of the political conflict that smolders in our increasingly fragmented postmodern political culture. As Hunter observes, "Culture wars always precede shooting wars," and, in light of current cultural warfare, "the possibility of conflict and violence should not surprise us" (1994, 4–5). Arthur Schlesinger (1998), though his overall tone is generally moderate and optimistic, also seems to sense such dangers when he warns of the separatism that he sees as promoted by more zealous advocates of multicultural education. According to Schlesinger, "Watching ethnic conflict tear one nation after another apart, one cannot look with complacency at proposals to divide the United States into distinct and immutable ethnic and racial communities, each taught to cherish its own apartness from the rest. One wonders: Will the center hold? or will the melting pot give way to the Tower of Babel?" (1998, 22).

Gray, taking a more global and far more apocalyptic view of cultural conflict, warns of the danger of "destroying civil society, of wrecking it in a frenzy of ideological or religious fervor" (1993, 326). He sees our "fragile institutions" as "being increasingly threatened by recent fundamentalisms and by the reemergence of atavistic ethnicities" (327). "The likely prospect, for most of the world in the coming century," according to Gray, "may well be terror and new forms of barbarism" (327).

Postmodernism and the Purposive State

What the postmodern condition presents us with, therefore, is a not entirely reassuring condition of radical pluralism: an extreme diversity of seemingly incompatible narratives, cultures, language games, and moral frameworks with no overarching criteria or framework by which one might be assessed as better or truer than the other. The political problem here is to find, as Gray puts it, "a sustainable *modus vivendi* among people having divergent world-views and value-perspectives that are rationally incommensurable—that is, whose differences cannot be settled by any kind of rational arbitration" (1993, vii–viii). If this assessment of our current political condition is correct, then it follows that an understanding of the state as a purposive association and of government as a teleocracy is inherently problematic and even potentially dangerous. The idea of a purposive state, after all, presumes the existence and the acceptance of some sort of grand narrative or story that somehow ties the substantive ends sought by the state to a betterment of the human condition, a story in which men and women are made "free" by the creation of wealth, by the equalization of wealth, by living in harmony with nature, or by following the will of some divinity. In contrast, the postmodern condition denies the possibility of precisely the type of shared grand political metanarrative that we can use to give common meaning to our political world.

When we seek to make sense of our lives in terms of a variety of different stories, when we speak in a variety of untranslatable tongues, the barriers to any meaningful sort of broad agreement on the substantive ends of the state and how best to accomplish them would seem daunting if not insurmountable. Indeed, the postmodern condition and its plethora of incommensurable language games call into question the very meaningfulness of any talk about substantive ends or purposes for a community. Such talk would seem to require precisely the type of a robust shared moral language that the postmodern condition denies to us.

What this means, therefore, is that in a state that is organized around a particular set of substantive purposes or ends, meaningful political discourse can take place only within the context of particular language games that can be used to specify more clearly those ends and alternative means of accomplishing them. In other words, political discourse in a purposive state will not and cannot reflect much, if any, in the way of universal values. Rather, such discourse must reflect the values of whatever cultural group or alliance of groups happens to be dominant at any particular time. Such a political discourse can have no place for those language games organized around other sets of ends, be they public or private, that are indifferent to or in conflict with the ends of those who hold power. This is because political discourse within a purposive association has no value unless it serves the ends of the state. In a community organized around economic development, for example, there may be little room in political discourse for language games that concern social justice or the preservation of nature. Similarly, in a community organized around the promotion of equality, less value will be placed on language games about individual liberty, enterprise, or self-reliance. Political discourse itself will be seen as having its purpose here solely in terms of producing effects that are consistent with the ends of the state. Michel Foucault saw perhaps most clearly the political implications of limitations on discourse when he argued that "the production of discourse is at once controlled, selected, organised and redistributed according to a certain number of procedures, whose role is to avert its powers and its dangers, to cope with chance events, to evade its ponderous, awesome materiality" (1972, 216). Foucault noted that the "prohibitions" surrounding speech "soon reveal its links with desire and power" (216).

This limitation on the range of language games that can be employed within the political discourse of a purposive association has especially important implications within the postmodern condition. It means that many individuals will be required by the teleocratic government of a purposive association to assume obligations or to follow prescriptions that are not recognized within the context of their own particular language games or that are inconsistent with the values they happen to hold. They may be required to contribute labor, to give up property, or to alter their conduct of behavior in significant ways for reasons that make little or no sense in terms of the worldview provided by their own language games. Furthermore, many individuals may find that what they perceive as wrongs done to them by government are simply not recognized as such within the dominant language games of the purposive state. There emerge more cases of what Lyotard calls a "differend," where the regulation of conflict between two parties "is done in the idiom of one of the parties while the wrong suffered by the other is not signified in that idiom" (1988, 9).

Finally, the danger exists that a greater number of individuals may be excluded altogether from participation in political discourse, that they will no longer really be regarded as members of the political community, that they will become marginalized and actually cease to have political obligations as such and become simply objects to be ignored, to be manipulated, or even to be disposed of by the dominant political community as it sees fit. In other words, the potential for political repression, which is ever present in a state constituted along the lines of purposive association, becomes significantly elevated because of the fragmented character of postmodern political culture. Lyotard seems to sense the danger here. He observes that the "we" in postmodern political discourse will be "condemned . . . to remain particular, to be you and me (perhaps), to leave many parties on the outside. . . . It will have to resign itself to the loss of unanimity" (Lyotard 1993, 26). Under such conditions, according to Lyotard, there is a significant risk that "terror," by which he means the threat of exclusion from the political community, would be exercised "for 'our' satisfaction, the satisfaction of a 'we' permanently restricted to its particularity" (27). Lyotard suggests that what is involved in this regard is "tyranny: the law 'we' proclaim is not addressed to *you*, fellow citizens, or even subjects; it is applied to *them*, the third parties on the outside, without the least concern for legitimating it in their eyes" (27).

The fragmented character of the postmodern culture increases the risks associated with the monist ways of thinking that, as has been argued here, so often characterize teleocratic approaches to governance and administration. It makes it more likely that human values seen as important by some groups will be trampled on in the overly zealous pursuit of whatever particular set of human ends are deemed to be important by government. Berlin was keenly aware of the dangers of this type of monism in government. He warned that "the possibility of a final solution—even if we forget the terrible sense that these words acquired in Hitler's day—turns out to be an illusion; and a very dangerous one. For if one really believes that such a solution is possible, then surely no cost would be too high to obtain it: to make mankind just and happy and creative and harmonious for ever" (Berlin 1992, 15).

In other words, monism or a belief in a single criterion of goodness or value can breed an extreme form of instrumental rationalism in which the ends may be used to justify almost any means. As Berlin observed, "If I know which way to drive the human caravan" and "you are ignorant of what I know, you cannot be allowed to have liberty of choice even within its narrowest limits, if the goal is to be reached" (1992, 15). Furthermore, "if there is resistance based on ignorance or malevolence, then it must be broken and hundreds of thousands may have to perish to make millions happy for all time" (15). As Berlin argued, the belief that "it is in principle possible to discover a harmonious pattern in which all values are reconciled, and that it is towards this unique goal that we must make" can lead not only to "absurdities in theory," but also to "barbarous consequences in practice" (1969, lv–lvi).

Postmodernism and the Rhetoric of Public Administration

In light of the above, it may be useful, at this point, to briefly revisit some of the rhetoric of public administration writers discussed earlier. In this way, we can see better perhaps how obstinately it seems to run against the current of postmodernity. Consider, for example, Leonard White's textbook definition of public administration as "the management of men and materials in the accomplishment of the purposes of the state" (1926, 2). Consider also, in the context of public administration, Luther Gulick's advocacy of "the development of intelligent singleness of purpose in the minds and wills of those who are working together as a group" (1937a, 6) or his approval of ever-advancing areas of "socially enforced coordination" (40). Such rhetoric would seem to take on a chilling tone in light of our fragmented political culture that, by its very nature, must reflect multiple, incommensurable, and conflicting purposes. Equally worrying is Herbert Simon's admonition that administrators should "take as their ethical premises the objectives that have been set for the organization" (1976, 52) and his reference to the "scheme of social values" that is to be imposed by "organized society" on "the individual . . . in place of his personal motives" (218). Of course, these writers are not totalitarians. They would, no doubt, bristle at any notion that they are seeking to impose their particular notion of what is good and true on others. Nonetheless, if their teleocratic approach to administration is to be taken seriously, then what would seem to be required is a clarity and a coherence in the purposes and values of public policy that can be attained in a postmodern political culture only by promoting purposes and values held by some political and cultural groups while at the same time ignoring or even trampling on the purposes and values held by others.

However, it is too easy here perhaps to take rhetorical potshots at the modernist rhetoric of early-twentieth-century writings from the vantage point of the postmodern political condition. After all, a reasonable argument can be made that their teleocratic approach to governance and administration was defensible at the time, that it made some kind of sense in the context of a national political culture, rendered necessarily more collectivist in its character by the almost apocalyptic combination of a wrenching economic depression and world war. What is more troubling is how little the teleocratic flavor of public administration rhetoric has changed over the past half a century despite the increasingly obvious fragmentation of our political culture. Contemporary public management writers, for example, as we have seen, continue to urge public administrators to focus their efforts on pursuing "critical missions," "important public policy goals," and "important public purposes," with little if any thought given to what, if anything at all, these terms might really mean in light of the plurality of incommensurable values and ends that make up the quilt of our postmodern political culture. In this regard, David Osborne and Ted Gaebler's almost militant advice to entrepreneurial leaders of government to "rally their communities to their visions" and to "overcome the opposition" to their visions (1993, 327) would seem quite oblivious to the radical diversity or pluralism of postmodern political culture.

Indeed, writing with Peter Plastrik, Osborne seems recently to display, whether intentionally or not, an almost complete lack of regard for political pluralism in general when he argues that reinventors of government need to "stand up to the interests that block change" by pursuing a "damn the torpedoes, full speed" approach to administrative and political reform (Osborne and Plastrik 1997, 329). Osborne and Plastrik cite, with obvious approval, the following advice of Roger Douglas, a New Zealand government minister: "Do not try to advance a step at a time. Define your objectives and move towards them by quantum leaps. Otherwise the interest groups will have time to mobilize and drag you down" (Osborne and Plastrik 1997, 330).

All of this advice is perhaps superficially attractive, and it can even be inspiring, like some revolutionary tome, especially to those political leaders and managers who are trying honestly to pursue what they see as publicly beneficial agendas for change. The problem, however, is that such advice presumes that the opponents of reform are merely obstinate obstructionists to be knocked out of the way on the path to collective self-improvement. It does not stop to consider whether such opponents might, in a pluralistic postmodern culture, be different groups of citizens seeking simply to try to protect values or ways of life that they happen to see as important to them and under attack.

If we accept, therefore, that we are in a postmodern condition, the type of teleocratic approach to governance and administration exhibited in much of the public administration literature seems simply inappropriate. Furthermore, to the extent that these writings actually influence practice, this approach is also potentially dangerous in that it encourages public administrators to think of their actions largely in terms of identifying and implementing a coherent set of substantive purposes on behalf of a community. In doing so, it encourages public administrators not only to accept but also to promote the domination of political discourse by language games that are useful to and that promote the interests and values of a narrow range of political subcultures as they seek to advance their ends at the expense of other subcultures. In other words, the rhetoric of public administration would seem to cast public administration into the role of an instrument of the purposes and values of whatever faction or coalition of factions happens to hold the reins of power in the middle of an ongoing cultural conflict.

Of course, one might argue here that, given the checks and balances of our constitutional form of governance, the likelihood of a teleocratic form of public administration being used in the service of repression is relatively small and that I have overstated the dangers of teleocracy. Certainly, as suggested in the previous chapter, it is true that the decentralization of political power that is promoted by our constitutional

POSTMODERNITY AND THE STATE IOI

system already presents a significant practical obstacle to those who would try to use public administration as an instrument for the sustained achievement of any coherent set of purposes. Nevertheless, my point here is not that a teleocratic public administration will somehow transform our liberal constitutional order into some sort of a totalitarian machine. I am simply suggesting that, with the emergence of the postmodern condition, it becomes increasingly likely that acts of public administrators, when directed toward the achievement of particular substantive purposes and values, will inevitably come to be seen as repressive by those who do not share these purposes and values. Furthermore, it should be recalled that our constitution has not always been able to prevent random oppressive and even violent acts of administration. David Rosenbloom and Rosemary O'Leary (1997) have noted some "spectacular" failures in administrative discretion even in the recent past: how, for example, during the early part of the cold war, the Atomic Energy Commission knowingly exposed populations downwind from atmospheric nuclear tests to radioactive fallout and how, from 1932 to 1972, the U.S. Public Health Service studied the effects of untreated syphilis on African American men while withholding from them any medical treatment or relief for their suffering (1997, 31). They also note "more mundane administrative failures," including "nationwide, illegal, health-threatening government disposal of toxic substances" and "shockingly wayward police behavior" (45). These examples may well be the exception rather than the rule, but they point to the potential dangers of an overly zealous pursuit of teleocracy in public administration.

Furthermore, even where individuals and groups are able to protect themselves, whether through the courts or through the legislature, from what they see as the repressive actions of public administrators, it is not unreasonable to suggest that a teleocratic approach to administration will heighten the level of conflict that already tears at the threads of our fragmented political culture. The clarification and specification of public purposes required of a truly teleocratic form of administration runs the risk of simply fanning the fires of postmodern political conflict. Old-time pluralist writers, such as Charles Lindblom (1959), who certainly cannot be thought of as postmodernists, have long argued that being specific about public policy ends and values tends to raise the level of political conflict and make agreement about policies more difficult. This tendency is clearly magnified in a postmodern political environment in which, as we have seen, there are deep and irresolvable conflicts among multiple ends and values.

Civil Association and the Postmodern Condition

The root problem of the idea of a state as a purposive association from a postmodern perspective is that it is based on a notion of the state as a unity or a totality, a state organized around a unified set of ends. Lyotard argues, however, that "the idea that I think we need today in order to make decisions in political matters cannot be the idea of the totality, or of the unity, of a body" but "can only be the idea of a multiplicity or of a diversity" (Lyotard and Thébaud 1985, 94). If this is correct, then it follows that the idea of a state as a purposive association is ill-suited to the postmodern condition. It is an attempt to impose a form of monism, a unified conception of what is good and true, in the midst of an extreme pluralism. What is required instead is a vision of the state and a corresponding style of governance and administration that recognizes the multiplicity and diversity of narratives, language games, or cultures characteristic of the postmodern condition, a vision that recognizes, as Berlin observed, that "the ends of men are many, and not all of them are in principle compatible with each other" so that "the possibility of conflict—and of tragedy—can never wholly be eliminated from human life, either personal or social" (1969, 169). Such an understanding is, in my view, at least intimated in the practice of civil association.

A vision of a state as a civil association would seem appropriate for the postmodern condition because civil association does not require that all individuals engage in a common political discourse organized around the identification of any particular ends of the state and how best to achieve them. As Richard Rorty has suggested, it is simply a vision of "society conceived as a band of eccentrics collaborating for the purposes of mutual protection rather than as a band of fellow spirits united by a common goal" (1989, 59). It is, in Rorty's words, an "ideal liberal society . . . one which has no purpose except freedom, no goal except a willingness to see how such encounters go and to abide by the outcome" (60).

As such, therefore, civil association does not require that individuals buy into a particular metanarrative of purposive association. It does not require that they engage only in those language games that are supportive of a particular vision of purposive association. Within a civil association, individuals may continue, of course, to engage in political discourse based on their own visions of purposive association with those who share these visions. They are limited, however, by the rules of civil association in their ability to impose their language games on those who have different visions of the state. Civil association, in other words, acts as a check on the monopolization of political discourse by narratives or language games that favor a particular vision of purposive association.

Civil association would seem in this way to permit the use of a broader or more diverse range of language games than is likely under purposive association. Indeed, as Oakeshott argues, "not having any substantive purpose of its own a state understood in these terms is inherently accommodating to all expressions of the associative propensities of its members" (1975, 314). It allows them "to enter into relationships of affection, of discourse, of gainful enterprise or of playful engagement, but in respect of being civilly associated they cannot be either required or forbidden to do so" (Oakeshott 1975, 314). Civil association provides, in Oakeshott's words, a "freedom" that "lies, first, in the associates *not* being related to one another in the pursuit of any substantive purpose they have not chosen for themselves and from which they cannot extricate themselves by a choice of their own, and secondly in their actions and utterances being not even officially noticed or noticeable (much less subjected to examination or direction) in respect of their substantive character" (1975, 314).

Civil association is, according to Oakeshott, the "least burdensome of all human relationships in terms of obligations to subscribe to noninstrumental rules of conduct" and "is the only kind that excludes no other and that mitigates conflict without imposing uniformity" (1991, 460). The link suggested here between Oakeshott's idea of civil association and postmodern political culture is also seen by Gray in his exposition of what he terms "postliberalism." Gray observes that "in the subtle mosaic of traditions which is modern society," government "cannot claim to express any deep, undergirding moral community in the society, since no such community exists" (1993, 264–265). In such societies, he argues, the task of government is "to keep in good repair . . . civil association—that structure of law in which, having no purpose in common, practitioners of different traditions may coexist in peace" (265). As Gray notes, "Where deep moral solidarity is lacking, where (as in all modern societies) there is cultural diversity rather than seamless community, the role of government is first and last that of preserving liberty in civil association under the rule of law. The liberty that is preserved is that of the liberal individual, but it is a liberty that thereby guarantees cultural freedom—the condition in which individuals may opt to explore an inherited form of life, or migrate across traditions to a chosen lifestyle, if they so wish" (265).

Civil association would seem better able than purposive association to deal with the sharp conflicts between incommensurable values that, as suggested above, become more prominent in a postmodern political culture. It permits a pluralism in values by providing a measure of what Berlin terms "negative liberty" so that individuals, as a rule, are free to resolve difficult and sometimes tragic conflicts between incommensurable values without the interference of government. As Berlin noted, pluralism, along with the negative liberty that it entails, is a more humane ideal because "it does not (as the system builders do) deprive men, in the name of some remote, or incoherent, ideal, of much that they have found to be indispensable to their life as unpredictably self-transforming human beings" (1969, 171). Pluralism also, according to Berlin, allows us the hope at least of maintaining "a precarious equilibrium that will prevent the occurrence of desperate situations, of intolerable choices—that is the first requirement for a decent society" (1992, 18).

In short, therefore, the idea of the state as a civil association would seem to fit quite well with the postmodern idea of a multiplicity and diversity of political subcultures, language games, and values. It would seem to square with Lyotard's argument that "every one of us belongs to several minorities" or "territories of language," and only when "none of them prevails" can we say that "society is just" (Lyotard and Thébaud 1985, 95). Obviously, even within a civil association, political discourse still requires some sort of common language that different subcultures can use in interacting, cooperating, or simply settling disputes with one another. Nonetheless, discourse across political subcultures within a civil association does not require the robust sort of language game requisite to the conduct of purposive association. A civil association requires, to use Rorty's terms, only that we "work out the details of the continually shifting compromises which make up the political discourse," and this, in turn, requires only "a banal moral vocabulary—a vocabulary which is no more relevant to one individual's private self-image than to another's" (1991a, 196). As Rorty argues, "Public dealings with our fellow citizens are not *supposed* to be Romantic or inventive; they are supposed to have the routine intelligibility of the marketplace or the courtroom" (196).

Constitutionalism and Postmodernism

The link suggested here between civil association and the postmodern condition is especially important for American public administration because of the influence of the idea of civil association within our own constitutional and political tradition. American constitutionalism as an expression of the idea of civil association has considerable relevance to the postmodern condition. The types of rules and institutions characteristic of American constitutional tradition can be seen as providing multiple veto points that limit the ability of particular political subcultures to monopolize political discourse within a postmodern political culture. By forcing these subcultures, as they seek their own ends, to accommodate themselves to others, seeking different ends, such veto points encourage the use of a greater number and variety of language games in shaping public policy actions. In doing so, they place some limit on the harm that these subcultures can do to each other. In this respect, whatever its shortcomings, the Constitution, with its various checks and balances, would seem to be just the type of liberal "machinery" that Berlin saw as important "to prevent people from doing each other too much harm" and to "giving each human group sufficient room to realize its own idiosyncratic, unique, particular ends without too much interference with the ends of others" (1992, 47).

The importance of liberal constitutional institutions from a postmodern perspective is also seen by Rorty, who points to the "practical advantages" of such institutions "in allowing individuals and cultures to get along together without intruding on each other's privacy, without meddling with each other's conceptions of the good" (1991b, 209). His belief in the "ideal liberal society" is based on his belief that the "historical facts" would "suggest that without the protection of something like the institutions of a bourgeois liberal society, people will be less able to work out their private salvations, create their private self-images, reweave their webs of belief and desire in the light of whatever new people and books they happen to encounter" (Rorty 1989, 84–85).

It should be emphasized here that to accept the relevance of civil association and constitutionalism to the postmodern condition does not require that we accept as "true" the various metanarratives or what Oakeshott terms the "ideologies" that have been used on occasion to legitimate this type of politics. Examples of such metanarratives include those provided by contractarian philosophers, such as John Locke (1939), and more recently by constitutional public choice economists, such as James Buchanan (1975), who seek to ground or justify the practices of civil association and constitutionalism in some sort of "science" of human action. Even the *Federalist Papers* may be seen as an attempt at providing such a metanarrative. These metanarratives or ideologies, as Oakeshott observed, "may be valuable" as a rhetorical device in giving a "sharpness of outline and precision to a political tradition" (1991, 55), and they may have "some positive benefit" in that they "reveal important hidden passages in the tradition" (58). Still, a political ideology can be no more than, in Oakeshott's words, an "abridgment" of a tradition, "a system of ideas abstracted from the manner in which people have become accustomed to go about the business of attending to the arrangements of their societies" or "a meditation upon a manner of politics" (51). In other words, the ideas of civil association and constitutionalism should not be seen as providing rule books or templates for political activity but rather simply as describing certain "habits" of political behavior that we have picked up over the centuries. It follows, therefore, that my attempts here to link civil association and constitutionalism with the postmodern condition should not be interpreted as an effort to ground or justify civil association or constitutionalism in an abstract or an absolute sense. My intention is only to draw our attention to them as habits that we have acquired in the practice of our politics and to suggest simply that such habits may have their usefulness in a postmodern political culture.

Furthermore, when we assert that civil association and constitutionalism are useful habits in a postmodern political culture, this is not to turn a blind eye to what are now seen as wrongs, such as the enslavement of African Americans or the expropriation and relocation of Native American tribes, that have been committed and even justified in the name of civil association and constitutionalism. Civil associations and constitutions are the creations of humanity and not of deities, and, as such, the rules they provide do not immunize us from what later may come to be regarded as mistakes. To put it another way, there are no "mistake-proof" traditions or habits. Also, it can be argued here that particular activities come to be seen as "wrongs" because they create what are seen as contradictions or incoherences within our traditions or within our language games. In other words, without traditions or habits, such as civil association and constitutionalism, there are no "wrongs" to be put right.

Conclusion

If the above analysis is correct, therefore, the teleocratic approach to governance and administration should be rejected not only on the practical ground that it is difficult, if not impossible, to achieve within our constitutional form of governance but also on the moral ground that, given the fragmented nature of postmodern political culture, such an approach invites administrative actions that sometimes ignore or, even worse, trample on ends and values that are seen as important by particular groups or subcultures within our society. At the very least, efforts to achieve the vision of a purposive state and a teleocracy would seem likely to intensify the high level of cultural and value conflict that characterizes our postmodern condition.

In critiquing the vision of purposive association and teleocracy as expressed in the public administration literature, I am not denying that administrative activity should be somewhat purposeful. Public administrators, after all, do have to deliver public services. Streets and parks have to be kept reasonably clean and tidy, lakes and rivers have to be kept reasonably clean and healthy, sick people have to be treated, and fires have to be put out, and all of this activity admittedly requires some sense of purpose. Nevertheless, we must not confuse a useful sense of purposefulness in action with the idea, promoted in much of our literature, that such purposes can, somehow, collectively constitute a coherent set of ends for government as a whole or that we can, therefore, seek to design public administration as an instrument for the accomplishment of national or community ends.

If public administration as a field of enquiry is to understand better the practice of public administration and to suggest possible improvements, then we should, in my view, reject the vision of public administration as the instrument of a purposive state. Instead, we need to begin to think about public administration in terms of a state as a civil association. By thinking about public administration in terms of a civil association we would take better account of the fragmented and limited nature of political power in the system of limited governance handed down to us through the centuries, and we would work in conjunction rather than in conflict with it. We would also be better able to deal with the increasing cultural diversity of postmodern political and social life in ways that minimize repression and mediate conflict.

7

Public Administration in a
Civil Association

What would a public administration rooted in the idea of civil association look like? In order to help provide an answer to this question, it is useful again to consult history. In particular, in this chapter, we shall examine the practices of the justices of the peace in Stuart England as well as the legacy they have helped to provide for American administrative practice. Such an examination is useful for the following reasons. First, this period was one of constitutional struggle between the king and Parliament during which the idea of a state as a civil association began to crystallize or to take on a more well-defined shape. As John Gray has argued, "At the level of practice, English liberalism at this time comprehended a strong assertion of parliamentary government under the rule of law against monarchical absolutism, together with an emphasis on freedom of association and private property. It was these aspects of English political experience that Locke theorized and embodied in his conception of *civil society*—the society of free men, equal under the rule of law, bound together by no common purpose but sharing a respect for each others' rights" (1995, 13).

By looking at the administrative practice of seventeenth-century England, we may be able, therefore, to gain a better sense of what kind of a public administration was seen by Locke and others as compatible with the emerging idea of a state constituted as a civil association. Furthermore, this was also the period of history during which the English began to colonize America in significant numbers, bringing along with them, of course, the governmental customs and practices of their homeland. As Samuel Huntington has argued, what they brought with them were "late medieval and Tudor political ideas, practices, and institutions" (1968, 96–97). These "patterns of thought and behavior which were established in the New World" helped to shape not only colonial but also present-day American political institutions (1968, 97). They included ideas concerning "the subordination of government to fundamental law, the intermingling of the legal and political realms, the balance of powers between Crown and Parliament, . . . [and] the vitality of local government authorities" (Huntington 1968, 96). An examination of Stuart administrative practice, therefore, is helpful in understanding ways in which the practice of civil association in seventeenth-century England has influenced American public administration.

Why look at the practices of the justices of the peace? Because it was they who were responsible, during the seventeenth century, for the local administration of the Crown's domestic policies. In marked contrast to today, where justices perform a relatively minor role in governmental affairs, the justices of the peace of Stuart England were the preeminent officials of county government. Acting sometimes as an entire body through their court of quarter sessions but more often in smaller groups and sometimes even alone, these men served as general-purpose administrators for their counties, for the most part overseeing and prodding lower officials. By examining their practices, we can gain important insights, then, into the character of English public administration during this period of history. This chapter will focus on the independence or autonomy that was exhibited by the justices in their practices as well as the juridical or legalistic manner in which they conducted their business. It will also seek to show how these same characteristics are revealed in much of contemporary American administrative practice. Finally, the value of independence and juridicism in American public administration will be examined in light of the fragmented postmodern political culture in which we currently find ourselves.

An examination of early English traditions of administrative practice admittedly runs rather against the grain of American public administration scholarship. American public administration writers have generally not been inclined much to draw on pre-nineteenth-century English traditions of practice for inspiration about what constitutes a desirable public administration. Indeed, to the contrary, Woodrow Wilson thought that the influence of English traditions on American public administration was more a burden to be discarded or a problem to be remedied than a heritage to be explored. He saw more to be gained by examining Continental rather than English practices of administration. Wilson believed that "the English system is too much like our own to be used to the most profit in illustration" (1887, 219), and he thought it "best on the whole to get entirely away from our own atmosphere and to be most careful in examining such systems as those of France and Germany" (219). In a similar vein, Leonard White argued that our English administrative inheritance was inadequate in light of "the modern social and economic environment in which administration operates" and "the insistent demand for a greater and greater degree of state intervention" (1926, 7). As will be shown here, however, it is by consulting our English traditions of practice that we may be better able to avoid the pitfalls of teleocratic political thinking and gain an understanding of the appropriate role of public administration within a civil association.

The Office of Justice of the Peace

Who then were the justices of the peace? Edward III originally created the office of the justice of the peace in order to extend his power and authority over his kingdom during a period of what was exceptional lawlessness in fourteenth-century England (Beard 1904). These officials were authorized, among other things, "to restrain the offenders, rioters, and all other barators, and to pursue, arrest, take, and chastise them according to their trespass or offense; and to cause them to be imprisoned and duly punished according to the law and customs of the realm, and according to that which to them shall seem best to do by their discretions and good advisement" (Beard 1904, 41).

The justices of the peace were appointed by the monarch as unpaid officials, and they were recruited largely from the rural, landowning middle classes. The intent here was, on the one hand, to help the king undercut the power of the great feudal lords, but, on the other hand, to avoid the heavy expense of a large Continental-style professional bureaucracy (Dibble 1965). Following their establishment, the justices had their jurisdiction and responsibilities gradually but continually expanded. This expansion occurred especially during the Tudor era when governments, pursuing mercantilist economic policies, assumed much greater responsibilities not only for maintaining order but also for the detailed regulation of industry and trade and for the care of the poor. The justices became Queen Elizabeth's "maids of all work" (Trevelyan 1942a, 169).

As a result, by the beginning of the seventeenth century and the reign of James I, the justices of the peace were far more than simply a hybrid of policemen and lower magistrates. Their numerous responsibilities included regulating weights and measures, collecting taxes, repairing roads and bridges, inspecting drainage, supervising poor relief, impressing conscripts into military service, setting wages and enforcing wage contracts, controlling prices, enforcing apprenticeship requirements for the various trades, distributing military pensions, supervising the wool trade, and licensing and inspecting alehouses (Notestein 1954; Willcox 1940). The justices also paid off informers, suppressed vice and illegal games such as skittles and shuffleboard, enforced church attendance, and harassed Catholics and, later on, other groups of nonconformists. In short, the justices provided an administrative apparatus by means of which increasingly powerful monarchs sought to intervene in nearly every aspect of the lives of their subjects. Contrary to the views of White and other American public administration writers, these gentry were not the custodians of some "laissez-faire" or "night-watchman" state. In fact, they helped the Crown in its attempts to enforce, in the words of the historian William Bradford Willcox, "a body of restrictions which would stagger the most ardent supporter of the New Deal" (1940, 134).

The justices received a stream of orders, instructions, and assignments from the Privy Council, the central administrative body in London, and they, in turn, informed the council of any serious troubles in their jurisdiction. The justices were not simply the passive instruments of London, however. They often responded on their own initiative to local grievances and complaints. Furthermore, they expressed the concerns and the interests of the county to London. As Willcox noted, "From the point of view of the central government, they were the instruments for almost any task," but "from the point of view of the people," they were also "policemen, judges, and general advisers to the neighborhood" as well as "spokesmen for the county" (1940, 55).

The justices of the peace were at their most visible when they presided over the quarter sessions of the county. Here, the justices, in their judicial work, would deal with what were generally minor breaches of the law such as petty larceny, assaults, forcible entries upon land, sheep-stealing, housebreaking, trespass, and, of course, witchcraft. They were also frequently drawn into what amounted to civil actions, which they often settled through a process of arbitration. Quarter sessions, however, also provided the forum for the discussion of the administrative business of the county. According to Anthony Fletcher, some of the "staple items" of the justices' administrative agenda included "the poor law, apprenticeship, bastardy cases, the regulation of alehouses, local taxation, bridges and highways and the management of the gaol and houses of correction" (1986, 89). Because of the considerable time taken up by criminal trials, justices were limited in their ability to deal with detailed administrative matters at quarter sessions. They were forced to act largely as a coordinating body, discussing and setting general policy for justices, acting outside of quarter sessions (Barnes 1961, 77–79). They also served as a board of appeals for those citizens wishing to contest the administrative actions of particular justices. It is important to note here that judicial and administrative matters were often mixed together. Grand juries at the quarter sessions, in addition to presenting indictments against defendants, for example, served as a means of airing grievances against all kinds of government policies and their administration. In the seventeenth century, they became, in Fletcher's words, "informants at sessions about matters seen to be of general import" (1986, 165).

The Independence of the Justices' Administration

The various histories of the seventeenth-century justices of the peace indicate that, although they were agents of the Crown, the justices also often exhibited considerable independence in the exercise of their responsibilities. Most well known perhaps was the opposition of many of them to the attempts by Charles I to raise money without parliamentary approval, a factor that may well have contributed to the English Civil War (Willcox 1940; Barnes 1961). The independence exercised by justices of the peace went far beyond just issues of taxation, however. This is shown, for example, in Margaret Gay Davies's research on the enforcement of the 1563 Statute of Artificers, which mandated apprenticeships for entry into a variety of different occupations and trades. Davies observed here "the apparent indifference of local authorities to evasions of the apprenticeship law" (1956, 164). According to Davies, the law was enforced "only when it met an urgent need of the local community or was in harmony with strong public sentiment" (162). More generally, Fletcher has argued that justices of the peace enforced the laws that were handed down from London more or less strictly according to their own interests and their own view of the county's interests. According to Fletcher, "The pace of government was the pace set by the local justices. The standards imposed were the standards they found acceptable and to which they could obtain a response from leading villagers. In the last resort the standards achieved were those they were sufficiently troubled to enforce" (1986, 142).

The fact that the justices controlled the pace of administration did not mean that the interests of the central government were always at variance with those of the justices of the peace. To the contrary, both the Privy Council and the justices were clearly very concerned and arguably obsessed with the need to maintain peace and order in the counties. Nevertheless, the justices were not always willing to accept the current policy priorities of central government, and, furthermore, the methods they used to address them were not always those pre-scribed. As Fletcher has noted, "Policies that rested on consensus—regarding alehouses, dearth or vagrancy, for example," were enforced, but "they were only enforced at the pace that each county bench judged to be necessary" (1986, 356).

This point is evidenced in the administration of the Poor Law. Al-though a 1597 statute mandated financial relief to the poor to be paid out of local poor rates, many justices, seeking to avoid the imposition of unwelcome new tax burdens, were slow to pressure parishes to levy these rates. They preferred to rely instead on voluntary alms, and in some cases they even delayed the imposition of rates by issuing licenses to beg. Nonetheless, as the plight of the poor worsened during a series of periodic food shortages in the first half of the century, more and more justices, fearing famine and social disorder, ordered the imposi-tion of rates so that poor relief became more general. "The final estab-lishment of the poor rate" was, according to Fletcher, "a triumph of local initiative, a response to felt need" (1986, 187).

Nor did the justices of the peace always exercise their discretion simply to slow down or to dilute the implementation of central gov-ernment policies. For example, they responded quite proactively when dealing with severe food shortages in the late 1640s, despite the ab-sence at that time of any central directives or pressures to intervene (Fletcher 1986, 199). In the county of Wiltshire, for instance, justices attempted to increase the food supply by restricting the purchase of barley to make ale by the county's most active maltster. The justices also mandated the public display and sale of all corn, and they further secured an agreement from farmers to reserve a portion of their barley for sale to the poor at a fixed price. In Fletcher's view, "Material from a number of counties suggests that the magistracy coped triumphantly" (1986, 199).

Not surprisingly, the independence exercised by justices was a frequent source of frustration for both the king and his ministers. Because the justices of the peace were unpaid officials providing what was essentially voluntary service, however, the ability of the Crown to bring pressure to bear on them was always limited. There were, it is true, occasional purges by the Crown, but typically the offending gentry were eventually reappointed because of the limited pool of suitable candidates within any one county. Thus, the effectiveness of Stuart monarchical governance hinged largely on the willingness of local justices themselves to carry out the policies of the Crown. As William Holdsworth, a prominent English legal scholar of the early twentieth century, put it, "Dismissal had very few terrors. It followed, therefore, that the service of these officials would not be very willing unless the policy, which the central government wished to pursue, was approved of by these officials; and that it would be almost impossible for the central government to secure the enforcement of a policy which they actively disliked" (1967, 60).

The Juridical Character of the Justices' Administration

In addition to the independence displayed by the justices, the historical evidence also indicates that the law and its various mechanisms had a profound effect on their practices. In applying and interpreting the numerous statutes handed down from London, the Stuart justices, like their predecessors, employed the principles of common law that had been built up over preceding centuries. These men saw their responsibilities primarily in terms of maintaining the peace through the enforcement of law rather than helping the Crown to achieve its particular policy objectives in an efficient and effective fashion (Holdsworth 1967, 59).

Furthermore, the justices conducted their formal administrative business by means of medieval common law processes and instruments, including juries, presentments, and indictments (Holdsworth 1967, 59). Indeed, in the absence of a paid professional bureaucracy, it was only through the law and its machinery that the justices could exercise formal control, when required, over the actions of constables, parish overseers, surveyors, and other local officials. Hence, for example, administrative problems such as a failure of the county to keep highways, bridges, or gaols in good repair were dealt with officially as legal actions brought in court against the local officials alleged to be responsible. As Sydney Webb and Beatrice Webb observed in their classic history of English local government, local governments and their officials were "one or other of them, always in the dock as defendants to criminal indictments, on which they were perpetually being fined" (1963, 308).

The juridical character of public administration under the justices of the peace is made evident in the text of popular handbooks written for justices of the time, most notably William Lambarde's *Eirenarcha*, first published in 1588, and Michael Dalton's *The Countrey Justice*, first published in 1622. Both Lambarde's and Dalton's handbooks indicate the centrality of the law to the justices' responsibilities. Lambarde noted how the justice of the peace should "containe himselfe within the lists of law" and "use his owne Discretion, but onely where both the law permitteth, and the present case requireth it" (1972, 65). Dalton, in a similar vein, argued that justices should not act "according to their own wils and affections" (1972, 5) but rather according to "the lawes, customes, and statutes of this realme, without respect of persons" (4). Both Lambarde's and Dalton's handbooks addressed themselves to the justices' work out of sessions, Dalton's work exclusively so. Still, they offered here no managerial advice at all to their fellow justices. Instead, what was provided was essentially an enumeration of the legal powers of the justices and the legal procedures that were to be followed in exercising those powers.

Therefore, although the justices were capable of exercising considerable discretion in following the directives of the Crown, this discretion was shaped and constrained by the juridical manner in which they were accustomed to conducting their activities. Moreover, the common law and its machinery did more than simply constrain the discretion of the justices. It also helped protect the justices in the exercise of their discretion. Indeed, it can be argued that the juridicism of the justices' administration was yet another reason why they were able to exercise considerable independence from the Crown. Provided that the justices acted according to the law and its procedures, there was little that the Privy Council could do to control their actions. As Holdsworth noted, the "ordinary every-day work" of the justices "was done under judicial forms which left them free to act independently so long as they obeyed the rules of the common law" (1967, 59).

Although the juridical character of the justices' work is being emphasized here, it is important to note that their juridicism was often tempered by a willingness to settle disputes informally. Justices acted frequently outside of their courts as mediators in the disputes arising in their counties. As Willcox noted, "A great deal was done outside, in quieter ways which have left no record, by bullying and cajoling, by letters to London, by rough diplomacy over the beer glass" (1940, 72).

The Legacy of the Stuart Justices' Administration

In assessing the legacy of the Stuart justices for contemporary American public administration, we obviously should not paint an overly romantic picture of these men or their actions. Many of them were undoubtedly incompetent, corrupt, or both, and even their resistance to Crown policies was often motivated by financial interest as much as constitutional principle. John Nef, in his economic history of the period, clearly expressed this view when he argued that the justices "often subordinated the king's interest to their own, by giving sparingly of their time to their official duties" and "by giving a lukewarm response to orders from the privy council if these orders interfered with their business projects" (1964, 10). Even in their own time, the justices were frequently the object of ridicule and satire. Furthermore, judged by contemporary standards, the laws that the justices enforced, such as those against adultery, bastardy, fornication, games, swearing, and vagrancy, were undoubtedly often oppressive. Moreover, the sentences that the justices handed out seem cruel and even barbaric to contemporary eyes. These punishments included public whipping, branding, the cutting off of ears, stocking, pillorying, the ducking stool, and, of course, transportation to the colonies.

Notwithstanding all of their faults, however, the justices' practices have provided an important legacy for public administration both within Britain and the United States. Many historians, particularly those of a more Whiggish bent, have seen the independence exhibited by the justices in responding to royal orders as constituting an effective impediment or block to the dictatorial aspirations of the Stuart monarchs. G. M. Trevelyan, for example, the popular English historian, expressed this view most forcefully when he argued that the justices of the Stuart era ensured "the failure of the Stuart Kings to establish a despotism" (1930, 22). According to Trevelyan, the "fate of England" was decided when "magisterial resistance to the Crown" became "one with the resistance of the whole nation" (22). Holdsworth similarly argued that the opposition of the justices to the Crown's policies was "fatal to the success of a scheme of royal absolutism" and also "perhaps the most important cause for the ultimate success of the Parliamentary opposition" (1967, 61). Also, according to Thomas Skyrme, the justices "played an important part in curbing royal supremacy and in ensuring that attempts by James I, and particularly Charles I, to establish a dictatorship were unsuccessful" (1994, 296). Even Nef here, despite his clearly critical view of the justices, conceded that "the failure of royal absolutism in England is partly explained by the fact that the machinery of government, inherited from the Middle Ages and developed during the sixteenth and early seventeenth centuries, did not permit the English king as easily as the French king to act counter to the wishes of his chief subjects" (1964, 8).

Closely related to this idea is the observation that the juridical manner in which the justices conducted their affairs contributed significantly to strengthening English commitment to the idea of the rule of law. Trevelyan, for example, argued that "the respect in which the English hold the law was generated not a little by this system of 'amateur justice'" (1942b, 143). Fletcher more recently has suggested that the proceedings of the justices' quarter sessions "embodied and gave expression to a rule of law that made possible the security of property and inheritance and that held together a society that was blatantly divided by huge differences of wealth" (1986, 87). Consistent with this view, J. H. Gleason has argued that the legal experience of the justices, most of whom received at least some legal education and some of whom also served in Parliament, may well have contributed to the "instinct" in English-speaking societies that governments should "act in accordance with the simple phrases but complex notion variously called the rule of law and due process" (1969, 122). According to Gleason, the "legacy" of the Stuart justices was "a legalistic attitude toward social administration" (122).

All of this history is clearly not without some significance for American public administration. Indeed, it is worth observing that the American colonists and their successors adopted the tradition of administrative independence and juridicism that the Stuart justices helped to protect. Alexis de Tocqueville, for example, was clearly struck by the highly decentralized nature of the system of public administration that he found in nineteenth-century America. He saw such decentralized administration as an important check on the potential tyranny of majority government. According to Tocqueville, "In the United States, the majority, though it often has a despot's tastes and instincts, still lacks the most improved instruments of tyranny" (1969, 262). Tocqueville noted specifically here the importance of the American justices of the peace, who "everywhere . . . share in the administration of township and county" (83). He argued that the justice of peace "brings with him" to administration "a taste for formalities and for publicity which renders him a most inconvenient instrument for a despotism" (76). Tocqueville also observed the juridical character of early-nineteenth-century American public administration. He noted that in the United States "an administrative order is almost always concealed under a judicial mandate; thereby it is all the more powerful, having that almost irresistible force which men accord to due process of law" (77).

Notwithstanding the massive growth of the administrative state since the writings of Tocqueville, there are signs that the Anglo-American tradition of administrative independence is still very much alive (Cook 1992; Spicer 1995). Local officials even today continue to exercise significant independence in administering state policies, as do also both state and local officials in administering the policies and programs of the federal government. Also, as John Rohr (1986), James Q. Wilson (1989), and others have observed, the constitutional separation of powers has meant that, even at the federal level of government, administrators are not simply the passive instruments of either the president or Congress. Rather, public administrators can and do exercise considerable independence by choosing among their different constitutional masters.

Furthermore, the English tradition of the rule of law promoted by the justices' practices has given contemporary American public administration a distinctly juridical character. It has encouraged our own practice of seeking to control public administration through both laws and administrative rules and procedures. Indeed, James Q. Wilson traces our peculiar faith in the power of rules to control bureaucracy to the writings of jurists such as Sir Edward Coke, who sought to limit the power of the Stuart kings by means of the common law. Partly as a result of these influences, according to Wilson, we rely "on rules to control the exercise of official judgement to a greater extent than any other industrialized democracy" (1989, 342). Steven Kelman, in a similar vein, argues that "no other country in the world prescribes such a detailed set of decision-making procedures for government agencies. Nor does any country provide for such extensive review by the courts. . . . No other country requires anything even resembling our panoply of public hearings, cross-examination of witnesses, posthearing comments, and statements of reasons" (1987, 97).

Furthermore, administrative practice in the United States is becoming, if anything, increasing juridical in character. David Rosenbloom and Rosemary O'Leary (1997), for example, have shown how, across the past half century or so, the growth of administrative law and the increasing proclivity of courts to intervene in the administration of government programs and services, most notably in the areas of environmental administration and the protection of individual rights, have radically changed the character of American public administration. These writers observe that public administration is now "heavily infused with legal requirements, subordinated to the rule of law, and subject to far-reaching judicial supervision" and that "a good deal of what agencies do is to manage the legal processes of rule-making, enforcement, and adjudication" (Rosenbloom and O'Leary 1997, 82). Rosenbloom and O'Leary see these changes as constituting "nothing less than a fundamental and revolutionary change in the role of law in public administrative practice" (304). When viewed from a longer-term historical perspective, however, these changes appear less revolutionary. They can, in fact, be seen as a continuation and a modification of our long-standing administrative tradition of administrative juridicism.

In summary, therefore, I would argue that the tradition of administrative independence and juridicism that the justices' practices helped to foster is revealed quite strongly in our own administrative practices. This Anglo-American tradition of public administration, however, is clearly at odds with the teleocratic approach to public administration that is advocated by many public administration writers. In marked contrast with our practices, as we have seen, public administration writers have often advocated strengthening the power of the president, as chief executive, over the activities of public administrators as a means of promoting more efficient and effective administration. Furthermore, in recent years, as we have also seen, a wave of criticism has been advanced against the rule-bound character of American public administration by public management writers and the self-proclaimed reinventors of government. Nonetheless, notwithstanding the arguments of these writers, there is good reason to believe that our traditions of administrative independence and administrative juridicism may be of special importance in our current postmodern political condition.

The Usefulness of Administrative Independence and Juridicism in Postmodernity

Although obviously subject to abuse, administrative independence is of value within a fragmented political culture because it constrains the ability of any political faction or coalition of factions within government to use administration as a tool to impose its purposes and values on others. In postmodern terminology, a significant degree of autonomy in administration can limit the degree to which any one group can monopolize political and administrative discourse and action. Indeed, it allows administrators the freedom to draw on different language games in thinking and talking about their actions. The interpretation of statutes by administrators provides an example of this freedom. Where, as is often the case, the language of a particular statute is vague and ambiguous, if administrators can exercise independence, then they need not feel compelled to follow the interpretation of the statute offered by any particular faction involved in its enactment. Rather, they are free to entertain alternative interpretations of its text, and in doing so they can limit the harm imposed by the statute on others. Furthermore, administrative independence is useful because, at least to the degree that public administration operates within a relatively open governmental system such as ours, such independence encourages the participation of a variety of different groups and organizations in administrative decision making. The power that administrators can exercise by virtue of their independence tends, in and of itself, to attract involvement in administrative decision making by those who believe themselves to be potentially affected by the actions of administrators (Long 1949; Wilson 1989). Independence in administration means that individuals, groups, and organizations have an additional access point, beyond elected officials, by which they can exercise influence over the public policy process as it affects them. As a result, the range of interests, purposes, and values represented in policy discussions will tend to be broader than would be true in the absence of administrative independence. This being the case, the monopolization of political discourse by particular political subcultures employing a narrow range of language games to support their ends becomes more difficult. In this respect, by enabling administrators to resist the power of political leaders and by encouraging broader participation by outsiders in policy discussions, independence in administration can be seen as making possible, and even encouraging to some degree, what David Farmer has termed "anti-administration" or "administration which is directed at negating administrative-bureaucratic power" (1998, 5).

Administrative independence is, of course, not without its own risks. Public administrators who can act independently to some degree of political leaders but who are zealously possessed of their own particular vision of a purposive state might arguably feel more inclined to impose this vision on others. Public administration writers such as Herman Finer (1941) have long warned of the dangers of an unfettered public administration. This problem of unfettered administration helps us understand why the juridicism of the Anglo-American tradition of administration is also important. Administrative juridicism, with its rules, procedures, hearings, appeals, and written records, it must be admitted, reduces the flexibility of administrators. In doing so, however, it also limits the ability of public administrators to steer government in the direction of any particular set of substantive purposes that they might personally wish to promote. As such, administrative juridicism acts as a check on corruption and hubris. Furthermore, it limits the ability of administrators to discriminate between different individuals and between different groups and, as a result, provides for a certain measure of procedural justice. Such procedural justice is not without its value within a postmodern political culture. Richard Rorty clearly sees this when he argues that the cultural diversity in which we find ourselves is "just the sort of situation that the Western liberal ideal of procedural justice was *designed* to deal with" (1991b, 209). He finds, for example, "cheering" the outcome of a case of a Native American who, having waited his turn in a queue for a kidney dialysis machine, was permitted to begin and continue treatment despite his heavy and eventually fatal drinking (204). Rorty believes that we should take "moral pride in the fact that our society hands such decisions over to the mechanisms of procedural justice" rather than making them "on the basis of political or financial clout, family membership, or the sympathies of those present" (205). In Rorty's view, "We do not really want doctors to differentiate between the values of the lives they are saving, any more than we want defense lawyers to worry too much about the innocence of their clients, or teachers to worry about which students will make the best use of the education they are offering. A society built around procedural justice needs agents who do not look too closely at such matters" (205).

Finally, to the extent that adequate opportunities are afforded for individuals and groups outside of the bureaucracy to participate in administrative hearings, to file objections to administrative rules, and to appeal against administrative decisions, juridicism in administration allows for the consideration of a broader range of interests, values, and worldviews and the use of a broader range of language games than would otherwise occur within the discourse of administration. In this regard, administrative juridicism, when properly structured, can be helpful in limiting the degree to which public administrators themselves monopolize administrative discourse by forcing them to confront and to accommodate the myriad conflicts in values and cultures that are characteristic of our postmodern condition.

Conclusion

The administrative practices of seventeenth-century English justices of the peace turn out, therefore, to have considerable relevance for American public administration in that they highlight what are both important and valuable aspects of our traditions of administrative practice, namely, administrative independence and administrative juridicism. In order for the benefits of administrative independence and administrative juridicism to be realized within a postmodern political culture, public administration requires, of course, a high degree of openness to participation by citizens. In this regard, although American public administration is by no means perfect, it does at least rank fairly well in comparison with other countries (Kelman 1987; Wilson 1989). Therefore, although we should avoid complaisance, we should, at the same time, recognize the value of our Anglo-American traditions of administrative independence and juridicism and be more than a little wary of proposals for administrative reform, such as those offered by reinventors of government, that could seriously erode them.

8

Implications for Public
Administration Enquiry

This book has shown that although writers in the field of public administration may pay little explicit attention to the idea of the state, their writings convey a strong intimation of a particular vision of the state, one that has a long lineage in the history of political thought and practice. This is a vision in which the state is seen as a purposive association, as an organization in the image, perhaps, of a church, a factory, an army, or a hospital, and in which government is seen as the manager of such an organization. It is a vision of the state as a group of citizens whose activities are organized and managed by a powerful teleocratic government on their behalf around the pursuit of some coherent set of substantive ends or purposes. This vision of a purposive state, as we have seen, has its roots in the growth of centralized monarchical power in emerging European nation-states, starting in the late fifteenth century, and most especially in the development of an administrative apparatus in service of that power. I have noted here particularly the example of eighteenth-century Prussian administration under the leadership of Frederick the Great as one that demonstrated for many, both at that time and later, the real possibility of an enlightened rational teleocracy that could, with the assistance of a powerful but subservient public administration, enhance the collective material and moral welfare of it subjects. As we have seen, this vision of a purposive state and of a teleocratic government has, since Sir Francis Bacon, captured the imagination of many political and social thinkers, including that of prominent public administration writers. Such a vision was especially appealing to early public administration writers as the role of government in the lives of its citizens began to expand apace and the need for administrative reform to support this role seemed apparent. Furthermore, it has continued to exert a powerful influence on the field of public administration, as can be discerned in the hardheaded positivism of Herbert Simon and his disciples, in the catchy antibureaucratic tomes of the new public management and reinventing government movement, and in the more radical claims made by some writers for political empowerment of bureaucratic workers and clients.

I have argued here, however, that the pursuit of such a teleocratic vision of governance and administration is likely to be impractical because our constitutional system of governance reflects not a vision of purposive association but rather one of civil association. This latter vision of the state is one in which men and women see themselves as bound together only in their subscription to a set of noninstrumental rules of conduct, rules that serve not to promote any particular substantive collective aspirations that any of them might happen to share but only to limit and help resolve the conflicts and collisions that are likely to arise between them as these individuals pursue, either alone or in concert with others, their own particular ends. Reflecting as strongly as it does this vision of civil association, our inherited system of constitutional governance can provide neither for the concentration of political power nor for the level of control and predictability of human action that is necessary to the running of an effective teleocracy. Furthermore, notwithstanding its practical limits, the pursuit of a vision of teleocratic governance and administration is also potentially dangerous, especially in light of the fragmented character of our postmodern political culture. This fragmentation of our political culture makes it more likely that, when government attempts to pursue a particular set of substantive ends or values, it will end up inflicting harm on those citizens who do not happen to share those ends. As I have argued here, our fragmented political culture might, therefore, be better served by our inherited institutions and traditions of civil association because these aim at no purpose other than simply helping us get along together despite the diversity of our ends and values. These institutions and traditions include our Constitution and our customs of administrative independence and administrative juridicism as handed down to us, in significant part, through the practices of seventeenth-century English local public administrators.

Public administration writers, then, need to break out of the grip of the vision of a purposive state and to draw more on our political and constitutional traditions of civil association. This argument should not be misinterpreted in any way as a call to tear down the American administrative state and replace it with antique seventeenth-century institutions of public administration. To the contrary, as noted in the previous chapter, the contemporary American administrative state can be seen as reflecting, in significant part, our traditions of thought and practice as a civil association. What is argued here is that public administration enquiry can be more helpful in guiding and improving practice in the future if it also draws on these traditions.

The Traditions of Civil Association and Effective Governance

The idea that public administration enquiry should draw more on our political and constitutional traditions is admittedly somewhat unorthodox. Indeed, where public administration writers have paid any attention to these traditions at all, they have typically been critical of them. In particular, many writers in the field have seen our Constitution, with its separation of powers, as a serious obstacle to effective governance and administration and even as a threat to the continued existence of the American state. Woodrow Wilson expressed such a view when, in criticizing the separation of powers, he argued that "the federal government lacks strength because its powers are divided, lacks promptness because its authorities are multiplied, lacks wieldiness because its processes are roundabout, lacks efficiency because its responsibility is indistinct and its action without competent direction" (1956, 206).

Wilson warned ominously here that the lack of "one supreme, ultimate head" in our constitutional scheme "in times of sudden exigency . . . might prove fatal—fatal either in breaking down the system or failing to meet the emergency" (186). Even pluralist writers, such as Robert Dahl and Charles Lindblom, although generally sympathetic to our democratic system, have argued that our particular constitutional structure of government "vastly increases the amount of bargaining that must take place before policies can be made" (1953, 335) and "increases the likelihood of situations in which one set of policies cancels out another" (344). Furthermore, as a result of our Constitution, they suggest, "there is little unified control over government bureaucracies by elected leaders" (341). These writers caution us that "if the survival of this country should ever come down to depend upon squeezing the utmost from our resources, and hence on reducing conflicting policies to a minimum, the stark alternatives would be failure—or a drastic change in the policy process" (348).

More recently, Stephen Skowronek, a writer in the "return to the state" movement, observes that the effect of trying to build a modern administrative apparatus in the midst of our constitutional traditions has been to render our administrative state "a hapless administrative giant," one that can "spawn bureaucratic goods and services" but that defies "authoritative control and direction" (1982, 290). He predicts that "the search for control and direction may yet persuade us to move beyond our unwieldy Constitution" (292). Finally, Richard Stillman has argued that our constitutional design, with its emphasis on checking power, "impedes developing stable administrative systems to carry out governmental goals by permitting delay, stalemates, cross-purposes in actions, and inefficiency" (1990, 165). According to Stillman, because of our constitutional traditions,

> clear, swift action that would benefit the majority and offer long-term payoffs to future generations are often infrequent and hard to come by because the system is so diffuse and open, without any prudently designed, stable administrative system. Well-placed minority veto groups have numerous opportunities to throw sand in the gears and to stymie collective action. At times, this has even brought America to the brink of national disaster as in the case of the Civil War or in World War Two when entrenched minorities prevented adequate advanced military preparations. In the late twentieth century, such delay can become even more perilous and deadly (165–166).

In short, if these writers are to be believed, our administrative state is severely crippled by our ancient constitutional traditions and, given a serious enough crisis, could even collapse beneath its own weight. Despite such warnings, however, the fact is that our administrative state has shown itself remarkably effective in wielding power across the past century or so, whether for good or ill, and it shows little signs of pending collapse. Notwithstanding the supposedly widespread disillusionment with our administrative state, its spending continues to grow by hundreds of billions of dollars every year; political debate about it focuses essentially on how fast it should grow rather than whether or not it should grow; and there is apparently no shortage of ideas among political candidates of all stripes as to how we might harness this supposedly hapless giant in pursuit of new political agendas. It is worth noting here that few critics of the administrative state go as far as advocating constitutional reform. Even Stillman concedes that the record of the American administrative state is "not all that bad," and he observes that it has outlasted "most of the Marxist states" (1998, 173).

Stillman wonders, however, "whether it will be all that good for the future survival of the United States" (1991, 70). He suggests that "the jury is still out" on the "seminal question" as to whether we will "need a European-style state . . . in the future" (1990, 166). Obviously, as emphasized in my critique of the purposive state, nobody can predict the future. It is even conceivable that the American state itself could disappear altogether, subsumed perhaps into some sort of liberal Kantian world order of transnational organizations (Fukuyama 1992) or, alternatively, perhaps into one of a number of competing regional global confederations (Huntington 1996). Nonetheless, assuming that the foreseeable future is probably one in which the United States will continue to exist but, at the same time, experience sharp internal political conflicts because of our fractured political culture, the most sensible strategy for public administration practice, in my view, is not to discard but rather to continue to draw on our traditions of civil association, including our constitutional traditions. Certainly, even for those concerned about the survivability of the American state, this seems hardly the appropriate time for our field to urge on our political and administrative leaders that they jettison these traditions and move henceforth toward more unified, corporate, and teleocratic structures of governance and administration. As we have seen, such a move runs the risk that public administration will be used in the service of repression or, at the very least, of magnifying political conflict in a cultural environment in which there are already deep and seemingly irresolvable differences among competing ends and values.

Some postmodernist writers might respond here that a reliance on our political and constitutional traditions places unnecessary limits on our thinking about public administration in a postmodern era. They might see such an approach as too conservative or too backward looking, robbing us of the ability and opportunity to think creatively about solutions to problems of governance and administration. Charles Fox and Hugh Miller, for example, have argued that "constitutionalism fails us because it is simply too conservative; it is reactionary in the noble but still fettering Burkean sense" (1995, 28). Fox and Miller are correct in their criticism, in my view, when an attempt is made, in defending a set of traditions, to canonize or to privilege particular texts or interpretations of history. As noted earlier, however, my attempts to link our traditions of civil association and constitutionalism with the postmodern condition do not require that we accept as "true" the various metanarratives or ideologies that have been presented in the past to legitimate this type of politics. My argument does not seek to justify civil association in any absolute or universal sense. We might accept, for example, a pluralist argument that there are incoherences, from a social scientific point of view, in the Madisonian design (Dahl 1956) or even a neo-Marxist thesis that our traditions of governance have emerged as a result of a sometimes ugly and violent class struggle (Moore 1966). Even if any of these points of view were true, however, my argument is simply that, despite their shabby history, some of the habits that we have acquired in the practice of our politics can still have practical value in administering government in our postmodern political culture.

Public Administration Discourse and the State

Whether or not the reader happens to share my particular sympathy for the traditions of civil association, the ideas presented here have important implications for public administration as a field of enquiry. In particular, my analysis of our literature indicates that public administration writers and teachers should pay a lot more attention than they have to the idea of the state. As demonstrated in this book, our ideas about the state are intimated in our discourse whether we choose to be explicit about them or, for that matter, whether we choose to be aware of them. That a lot of the supposedly apolitical theories and arguments of public administration writers should turn out to be not so apolitical after all should probably not surprise us. As indicated at the beginning of this book, the moral and political values we happen to hold permeate the mental categories or the presuppositions that we bring to the examination of the "facts" of human action and experience, including the "facts" of public administration. These categories shape the very language that we use to talk and write about public administration. How we choose to describe and make sense of public administration, then, inevitably reflects our values and is tied to what sort of institution we think government is, can be, or ought to be. To put it another way, there is no Archimedean point from which we can look at public administration, freed of our moral and political presuppositions. As Isaiah

Berlin observed, "Those who are concerned with human affairs are committed to the use of moral categories and concepts which normal language incorporates and expresses" (1969, 115). In light of this point, theorizing about public administration would seem, almost inevitably, to involve our ideas about morals and hence also about politics. As Dwight Waldo has argued, it is in "limited, technical areas where public administrationists can escape, practically speaking, from concern with political theory; but, nevertheless, in their central concerns they cannot avoid this encounter" (1984, lvii).

Neither does the devotion of many in the field to the canons of a value-free science of public administration and policy eliminate the political theory that is intimated in much of their discourse. Indeed, a belief that the major problems of governance and administration can be resolved using value-free social science itself reveals not the absence of any political theory but rather the presence of a particular type of political theory. A belief that the major problems of public administration are technical and subject to scientific resolution reflects itself a form of political theorizing. As Waldo argued with respect to the early advocates of a more scientific approach to administration, "Far from removing themselves from the realm of political theory, as many appear to believe, this devotion to a concept of reality called Science makes students of administration part of a well-known company of political theorists" (1984, 21). In this respect, then, we must accept that the distinctions we have periodically drawn in our field between "politics" and "administration" and between "facts" and "values," although by no means meaningless, can never be absolute and that moral and political ideas will inevitably affect our enquiries concerning human actions in public administration no matter how hard we might try to remove them.

The above argument does not mean, of course, that we are always compelled to moralize. Nor should we abandon our standards of fairness or objectivity in looking at the facts of public administration. Fairness and objectivity are, at the very least, useful habits of thought that we have come to realize are important in many aspects of our lives. Nonetheless, we should not seek, in the pursuit of a value-free science of administration, to expunge all notions of morality and values from our thinking and from our vocabulary. In an applied field such as public administration, we have to come to terms with the fact that we are somewhat more like historians than physicists. Hence, we cannot avoid as a rule the use of what Berlin terms "normal language with all its associations and 'built-in' moral categories" (1969, 115). We should try, therefore, as David Farmer (1995) and others have urged us, to be more self-conscious about the language we use in public administration and to reflect more on and try to understand the moral and political ideas that are implicit in much of the language we use to talk about the "facts" of public administration.

Admittedly, the promotion of this type of self-consciousness concerning our moral and political ideas is not an easy task. It requires that public administration writers explore and draw much more than they have on the ideas of political philosophy. Examination of political philosophy cannot, of course, provide us with a "correct" model of administration. It cannot per se tell us what public administrators should or should not do. Nevertheless, consulting political philosophy can make clearer for us the political and moral implications of the administrative ideas that we espouse and the administrative practices that we choose to follow. Furthermore, such consultation can help us understand where and why these theories and practices are likely to come into conflict with each other and, equally important, where and why they may conflict with the political and moral values of our culture. In addition, greater self-awareness of our political and moral ideas also requires that we pay more attention to the history of government and public administration so as to understand the context of our ideas and the ways in which our evolving political and administrative practices have reflected these ideas over time. History here can help us better understand the political and moral ideas that we currently happen to hold by drawing our attention to the more concrete details and nuances of the human practices from which they emerged and how these have shaped our thinking.

Finally, we should also examine the political and administrative practices and ideas of other countries. Such an examination can be useful in understanding how political and administrative practices are shaped by the different ideas that people living in different countries hold about politics and the state. Looking carefully at the experience of other countries may help us overcome our proclivity to search for the holy grail of a set of universal, value-free "principles of administration" applicable to all peoples and all times. In this regard, we should never engage in the comparative study of administration in a frenzied search for "best practices," as reinventors, for example, often seem to urge us to do. Each country's governmental practices and thinking are shaped by its own particular moral and political ideas so that administrative practices cannot be simply transferred from one country to another (Rosenbloom 1999). Rather, the primary value of a comparative perspective may lie, perhaps paradoxically, in providing us a contrasting perspective by which we can understand more clearly our own moral and political ideas and the way in which they have shaped our administrative practice and thought. As Oakeshott put it, "To range the world in order to select the 'best' of the practices and purposes of others . . . is a corrupting enterprise and one of the surest ways of losing one's political balance; but to investigate the concrete manner in which another people goes about the business of attending to its arrangements may reveal significant passages in our own tradition which might otherwise remain hidden" (1991, 64–65).

Some may object here that the pursuit of a more philosophical, historical, and comparative approach to public administration runs the risk of rendering it too theoretical and too far removed from the present-day concerns of practicing public administrators. This suggestion, however, ignores the fact that the moral and political ideas that we expound in our writings and in our classes, whether consciously or unconsciously, can have practical consequences. In particular, if we are not self-conscious about our own moral and political ideas, then we run the risk that public administration may become captive to ideas that are destructive of values we hold dear. As Berlin noted, "Men cannot live without seeking to describe and explain the universe to themselves. The models they use in doing this must deeply affect their lives, not least when they are unconscious; much of the misery and frustration of men is due to the mechanical or unconscious, as well as deliberate, application of models where they do not work" (1979, 10).

Indeed, a good argument can be made that it is precisely when we seek to exclude a discussion of moral and political values from our discourse that our thinking about governance and public administration can become most dangerous. This is because, in excluding moral and political discourse, we are more likely to lose sight of the reality that many of our important values, such as liberty and equality, justice and compassion, are often incompatible and in conflict with each other and that carefully considered compromises between them are necessary to prevent us from doing too much damage to any one of them. In not thinking consciously about our values and the conflicts that arise between them, public administrators, as well as the professors who often teach them, risk falling prey to that extreme form of instrumental rationalism in which a given set of ends prescribed by political leaders may be used to justify almost any means (Adams and Balfour 1998).

Public Administration and Civil Association

Regardless, therefore, of whatever political and moral ideas undergird each of our own particular enquiries into public administration, there is much to be said for encouraging a greater self-awareness of these ideas. I have argued in this book that the idea of the state as a civil association may be helpful to us in public administration in light of our constitutional and political traditions and the postmodern fragmentation of our political culture. If this argument is correct, then we would profit particularly by learning to talk and write about public administration in a manner that is more coherent with, or resonates more with, our political and constitutional habits of civil association. In order to do this, however, we need to come to terms with what civil association is really about. What is of central importance here, in my view, is that we accept, as our point of departure, the diverse nature of human ends and activities that are characteristic of a civil association. Michael Oakeshott captured this idea of diversity when he observed that, within a state thought of as a civil association,

> the situation to which the activity of governing has to be related is . . . something like this. I and my neighbours, my associates, my friends and my compatriots, are people engaged in a great variety of activities. We are apt to entertain a multiplicity of opinions on every conceivable subject and are disposed to change these beliefs as we grow tired of them or as they prove unserviceable. Each of us is pursuing a course of his own; and there is no project so unlikely that somebody will not be found to engage in it, no enterprise so foolish that somebody will not undertake it. We are all inclined to be passionate about our own concerns, whether it is making things or selling them, whether it is business or sport, religion or learning. . . . We enter into relationships of interest, of emotion, of competition, partnership, guardianship, love, friendship, jealousy and hatred, some of which are more durable than others. We make agreements with one another, we have expectations about one another's conduct; we approve, we are indifferent and we disapprove (1993, 48).

What we must accept, therefore, is that within a civil association men and women will pursue a great variety of different activities and ends, some of them with great passion, and that not all of these will make sense to all of us. Furthermore, we have no reason to believe that these diverse activities and ends will always or even generally be in harmony with one another. On the contrary, as Oakeshott argued, "This multiplicity of activity and variety of opinion is apt to produce collisions: we pursue courses which cut across those of others, and we do not all approve of the same sort of conduct" (1993, 48).

Admittedly, accepting this condition of a diversity of human ends and activities may not always be easy within the field of public administration, particularly for those writers of a more managerial or a more analytical bent. This is because such diversity often brings with it the appearance of disorder: an uncomfortable untidiness, if not actual chaos. Oakeshott acknowledged this when he observed that "surveying the scene, some people are provoked by the absence of order and coherence which appears to them to be its dominant feature; its wastefulness, its frustration, its dissipation of human energy, its lack not merely of a premeditated destination but even of any discernible direction of movement. It provides an excitement similar to that of a stock-car race; but it has none of the satisfaction of a well-conducted business enterprise" (1991, 425).

In this respect, acceptance of diversity as our current condition means letting go of the feeling, in Oakeshott's words, that there is "something that ought to be done to convert this so-called chaos into order" (1991, 426). It means putting aside dreams or visions of "the glorious, collisionless manner of living proper to all mankind," of "a condition of human circumstance from which the occasion of conflict has been removed," and "of human activity co-ordinated and set going in a single direction and of every resource being used to the full" (Oakeshott 1991, 426). It means, in short, putting aside teleocratic visions of governance and administration.

An acceptance of our current condition as one of a diversity of ends and activities, along with all the apparent disorder and chaos that this presents, is, in my view, fundamental to viewing public administration in the terms of a civil association. Such an acceptance is necessary in order to recognize clearly the key role that government must play as an arbitrator or umpire within our civil association and the contribution that public administration, as an institution, must make to that role.

Public administrators, as we have seen, exercise considerable discretionary power within our system of governance. They make independent judgments with respect to both the application of coercive power against citizens and the rationing of government services among them. As a result, the actions of administrators have the potential either to exacerbate or to help resolve what Oakeshott terms "the massive collisions which our manner of living is apt to generate and to release us from the massive frustrations in which we are apt to become locked" (1991, 429). In light of this potential, public administration as a field of enquiry needs to focus on the role that public administration can play in arbitrating political conflict within our civil association.

The foregoing suggests that public administration enquiry might benefit by drawing more on research from the field of conflict resolution. Certainly, this is the view of Zhiyong Lan, who argues that "in a post-industrial age in which cultures clash, political groups contend, gender and ethnic awareness awaken, and citizens' expectations of the government rise while willingness to pay for its services declines, a conflict resolution perspective gives us a conceptual tool to help with the task of 'reconciling the irreconcilable'" (1997, 33).

According to Lan, a variety of approaches to conflict resolution can be taken, administrative, political, and legal. Given our particular tradition of juridical administration and the increasingly important role that the law and courts play within public administration, however, public administration enquiry should pay special attention to the law and especially to administrative law as a major tool that we use to help resolve conflict within our civil association. As is true for political philosophy and history, law has been relatively neglected within the public administration literature. Although administrative law is a recognized subfield within public administration, as David Rosenbloom and Rosemary O'Leary have argued, "little effort is made to show how it both circumscribes and empowers public management" (1997, 51). As they observe, "As a field study, American public administration has been slow to recognize the importance of law to administrative practice" (83). Nonetheless, law is central to the resolution of conflict by government and public administration within a civil association because, as Oakeshott argued, the citizens of a state, conceived in the terms of a civil association, "have no use for an referee who does not govern the game according to the rules" (1991, 433).

In addition to the law, if public administration enquiry is to reflect more the idea of a state as a civil association, it should also draw more on our constitutional traditions. What is needed here is a continuing examination of our constitutional ideas and practices and their implications for public administration. The Constitution, after all, forms an essential part of the larger set of rules of our civil association and the part that is most relevant to the actions of public administrators. A sophisticated understanding of constitutionalism would seem essential to the practice of public administration within a civil association, and public administration as a field of enquiry should contribute to that understanding. Such an understanding cannot provide a rule book for the practice of public administration, but it can at least provide guidance for practitioners with respect to the type of role they should play within our civil association.

It must candidly be observed that, with some notable exceptions, public administration writers have tended to neglect our constitutional traditions (Spicer 1995). John Rohr (1986) and the so-called Blacksburg School (Wamsley et al. 1990) must be credited in this regard with providing a major advance in our thinking by seeking to analyze the practices of the modern administrative state in terms of the political thought of the founders. Rohr's idea of public administration as a "balance wheel" choosing among its constitutional masters would seem especially germane if the public administrator is to serve as a mediator of political conflict within our civil association.

If an examination of our constitutional heritage is to inform our understanding of a civil association, however, it is also important that we should not be seduced by attempts to enlist what remains of its prestige in the support of visions of the state that are antithetical to the idea of a civil association. Dale Wright and David Hart, for example, recently draw from the founders' writings the remarkable idea that it is the responsibility of the modern state somehow "to educate all citizens in the nature of civic virtue and then to persuade them to make that virtue the center of their personal character" (Wright and Hart 1996, 25). According to these authors, the "primary purpose [of government] is to facilitate the fully human life" that is "attainable only through living a life of virtue" (Hart and Wright 1998, 417). "All citizens," in their view, "must construct their personal, social, economic, and civic lives around the civic virtues" of "prudence, temperance, courage, and justice," of "faith, hope and charity," and of "moral exemplariness, extensive benevolence" and "self-sacrifice for the good of the polity" (416). In Hart and Wright's reading of our constitutional traditions, the founders' idea of the state as a civil association and of government as an arbitrator among competing ends and values would seem almost entirely lost. What is intimated in its place is a vision of the state as something like a church intent on the moral development of its members, if not the actual salvation of their souls. As a result, their analysis does little to further our understanding of the appropriate role of public administration within a civil association.

A more useful example of how constitutional theory can be used to gain insight into how public administration should operate within a civil association is provided by Douglas Morgan. In Morgan's constitutional analysis, the role of public administration is seen ideally as maintaining "balance among the competing claims of the majority, the protection of minority rights, and the competent performance of the tasks it undertakes" (1996, 45). He recognizes that, because of our constitutional legacy, "*how* we engage in governance is frequently as important as what those engagements produce in terms of tangible outcomes" (45). Morgan further understands and appreciates the "tendency of our rule-of-law system to transform narrow political differences into questions of legality and constitutionality" (45). Morgan's analysis reveals here a subtle understanding of the way in which the founders' idea of the state as a civil association undergirds our constitutional thinking and practices.

In consulting our traditions of civil association, however, we need not and should not confine ourselves solely to an examination of American constitutional thought and practice. It is also important to examine those British ideas and practices that have contributed to American constitutionalism. As the history of the Stuart justices of the peace makes clear, such an examination can be helpful in drawing our attention to and emphasizing aspects of our traditions of governance and administration that we might otherwise miss. Special attention should be paid here to the writings of such British political theorists as John Locke, David Hume, and Edmund Burke, whose ideas on the nature and politics of civil association both parallel and complement those of the founders.

Conclusion

In short, if public administration enquiry is to provide insight into the role of public administration within a state conceived as a civil association, it needs to draw on a much broader area of knowledge than is currently the case. It needs to go beyond the confines of mainstream empirical social science and embrace the fields of political theory, history, comparative government, and law. It needs to draw on our constitutional ideas and practices of civil association. Only in this way can public administration enquiry effectively transcend the politics-administration and fact-value dichotomies that have diverted the attention of so many in the field away from the relationship between public administration and the character of the state in which it operates. In this regard, Waldo's challenge to public administration orthodoxy set forth some half a century ago would still seem germane: "If abandonment of the politics-administration formula is taken seriously, if the demands of the present world civilization upon public administration are met, administrative thought must establish a working relationship with every major province in the realm of human learning" (Waldo 1984, 203).

References

Adams, Guy B. 1992. "Enthralled with Modernity: The Historical Context of Knowledge and Theory Development in Public Administration." *Public Administration Review* 52:363–373.

Adams, Guy B., and Danny L. Balfour. 1998. *Unmasking Administrative Evil*. Thousand Oaks, Calif.: Sage Publications.

American Economic Association. 1887. *Publications of the American Economic Association* 1.

Bacon, Francis. 1939a. "The Great Instauration." In *The English Philosophers from Bacon to Mill*, edited by Edwin A. Burtt. New York: Random House.

———. 1939b. "Novum Organum." In *The English Philosophers from Bacon to Mill*, edited by Edwin A. Burtt. New York: Random House.

———. 1942. *Essays and New Atlantis*. Roslyn, N.Y.: Walter J. Black.

Banta, Martha. 1993. *Taylored Lives: Narrative Production in the Age of Taylor, Weblen, and Ford*. Chicago: University of Chicago Press.

Barker, J. Ellis. 1916. *The Foundations of Germany: A Documentary Account Revealing the Causes of Her Strength, Wealth and Efficiency*. New York: E. P. Dutton.

Barnes, Thomas Garden. 1961. *Somerset 1625–1640: A County's Government during the "Personal Rule."* London: Oxford University Press.

Barzelay, Michael. 1994. "The Post-Bureaucratic Paradigm in Historical Perspective." In *Current Issues in Public Administration*, edited by Frederick S. Lane. New York: St. Martin's Press.

Beard, Charles. 1904. *The Office of Justice of the Peace in England*. New York: Burt Franklin.

Beloff, Max. 1962. *The Age of Absolutism: 1660–1815*. New York: Harper Torchbooks.

Behn, Robert D. 1995. "The Big Questions of Public Management." *Public Administration Review* 55:313–325.

———. 1998. "What Right Do Public Managers Have to Lead?" *Public Administration Review* 58:209–224.

Berlin, Isaiah. 1969. *Four Essays on Liberty*. New York: Oxford University Press.

———. 1979. *Concepts and Categories.* New York: Viking Press.

———. 1982. *Against the Current.* New York: Penguin Books.

———. 1992. *The Crooked Timber of Humanity.* New York: Vintage Books.

Bluntschli, Johann K. 1895. *The Theory of the State.* Oxford: Clarendon Press.

Brownlow, Louis, Charles E. Merriam, and Luther Gulick. 1997. "Report of the President's Committee on Administrative Management." In *Classics of Public Administration,* 4th ed., edited by Jay M. Shafritz and Albert C. Hyde. Fort Worth, Tex.: Harcourt Brace.

Buchanan, James M. 1975. *The Limits of Liberty: Between Anarchy and Leviathan.* Chicago: University of Chicago Press.

———. 1979. *What Should Economists Do?* Indianapolis: Liberty Press.

Burke, Edmund. 1955. *Reflections on the Revolution in France.* Indianapolis: Bobbs-Merrill.

———. 1992. *Further Reflections on the Revolution in France.* Indianapolis: Liberty Press.

———. 1999. *The Portable Edmund Burke.* New York: Penguin Books.

Carey, Henry C. 1967. *The Unity of Law.* New York: Augustus M. Kelley.

Carroll, James D. 1995. "The Rhetoric of Reform and Political Reality in the National Performance Review." *Public Administration Review* 55:302–312.

Catron, Bayard L., and Michael M. Harmon. 1981. "Action Theory in Practice." *Public Administration Review* 41:535–541.

Church, William F., ed. 1969. *The Impact of Absolutism in France: National Experience under Richelieu, Mazarin, and Louis XIV.* New York: John Wiley and Sons.

Cohen, Steven. 1988. *The Effective Public Manager: Achieving Success in Government.* San Francisco: Jossey-Bass.

Cook, Brian J. 1992. "Subordination or Independence for Administrators? The Decision of 1789 Reexamined." *Public Administration Review* 52:497–503.

Croly, Herbert. 1965. *The Promise of American Life.* Cambridge: Harvard University Press.

Dahl, Richard A. 1956. *A Preface to Democratic Theory.* Chicago: University of Chicago Press.

Dahl, Richard A., and Charles E. Lindblom. 1953. *Politics, Economics, and Welfare.* New York: Harper Torchbooks.

Dalton, Michael. 1972. *The Countrey Justice.* New York: Arno Press.

Davies, Margaret Gay. 1956. *The Enforcement of English Apprenticeship, 1563–1642.* Cambridge, Mass.: Harvard University Press.

Denhardt, Robert D. 1981. "Toward a Critical Theory of Public Administration." *Public Administration Review* 41:628–635.

Dennison, Henry. 1937. "The Need for the Development of Political Science Engineering." In *Papers on the Science of Administration,* edited by Luther Gulick and L. Urwick. New York: Institute of Public Administration.

Dibble, Vernon K. 1965. "The Organization of Traditional Authority: English Local Government, 1558 to 1640." In *Handbook of Organizations,* edited by James G. March. Chicago: Rand McNally.

DiIulio, John J., Jr. 1989. "Recovering the Public Management Variable: Lessons from Schools, Prisons, and Armies." *Public Administration Review* 49:127–133.

Dorn, Walter L. 1931. "The Prussian Bureaucracy in the Eighteenth Century." *Political Science Quarterly* 46:403–423.

———. 1932a. "The Prussian Bureaucracy in the Eighteenth Century II." *Political Science Quarterly* 47:75–94.

———. 1932b. "The Prussian Bureaucracy in the Eighteenth Century III." *Political Science Quarterly* 47:259–273.

Dyson, Kenneth H. F. 1980. *The State Tradition in Western Europe: A Study of an Idea and Institution.* New York: Oxford University Press.

Evans, Peter B., Dietrich Rueschemeyer, and Theda Skocpol, eds. 1985. *Bringing the State Back In.* Cambridge: Cambridge University Press.

Farmer, David J. 1995. *Language and Public Administration: Bureaucracy, Modernity, and Postmodernity.* Tuscaloosa, Ala.: University of Alabama Press.

Farmer, David J., ed. 1998. *Papers on the Art of Anti-Administration.* Burke, Va.: Chatelaine Press.

Finer, Herman. 1941. "Administrative Responsibility in Democratic Government." *Public Administration Review* 1:335–350.

Fletcher, Anthony. 1986. *Reform in the Provinces: The Government of Stuart England.* New Haven, Conn.: Yale University Press.

Follett, Mary Parker. 1937. "The Process of Control." In *Papers on the Science of Administration,* edited by Luther Gulick and L. Urwick. New York: Institute of Public Administration.

———. 1965. *The New State.* Gloucester, Mass.: Peter Smith.

Foucault, Michel. 1972. *The Archaeology of Knowledge and the Discourse on Language.* Translated by A. M. Sheridan Smith. New York: Pantheon Books.

———. 1977. *Discipline and Punish: The Birth of the Prison.* Translated by Alan Sheridan. New York: Vintage Books.

———. 1980. *Power/Knowledge: Selected Interviews and Writings.* Translated by Colin Gordon and others. New York: Pantheon Books.

———. 1988. *Politics, Philosophy, Culture: Interviews and Other Writings.* Translated by Alan Sheridan and others. New York: Routledge.

———. 1991. "Governmentality." In *The Foucault Effect: Studies in Governmentality,* edited by Graham Burchell, Colin Gordon, and Peter Miller. Chicago: University of Chicago Press.

Fox, Charles J., and Hugh T. Miller. 1995. *Postmodern Public Administration: Toward Discourse.* Thousand Oaks, Calif.: Sage Publications.

Frederick II, King of Prussia. 1789. *The Posthumous Works of Frederick the Great, Volume 5.* Translated by Thomas Holcroft. London: G. G. J. and J. Robinson.

———. 1966. *Frederick the Great on the Art of War.* Translated by J. Luvaas. New York: Free Press.

Frederick of Prussia. 1981. *Anti-Machiavel.* Translated by Paul Sonnino. Athens, Ohio: Ohio University Press.

Frederickson, H. George. 1971. "Toward a New Public Administration." In *Toward a New Public Administration: The Minnowbrook Perspective,* edited by Frank Marini. Scranton, Penn.: Chandler Publishing.

Fry, Brian R. 1989. *Mastering Public Administration: From Max Weber to Dwight Waldo.* Chatham, N.J.: Chatham House Publishers.

Fukuyama, Francis. 1992. *The End of History and the Last Man.* New York: Avon Books.

Gleason, J. H. 1969. *The Justices of the Peace in England, 1558–1640.* Oxford: Clarendon Press.

Gooch, G. P. 1990. *Frederick the Great: The Ruler, the Writer, the Man.* New York: Dorset Press.

Gore, Al. 1993. *From Red Tape to Results: Creating a Government That Works Better and Costs Less.* Washington, D.C.: Government Printing Office.

———. 1995. *Common Sense Government: Works Better and Costs Less.* New York: Random House.

Gray, John. 1993. *Post-Liberalism: Studies in Political Thought.* New York: Routledge.

——. 1995. *Liberalism.* 2d ed. Minneapolis: University of Minnesota Press.

Gulick, Luther. 1937a. "Notes on the Theory of Organization." In *Papers on the Science of Administration*, edited by Luther Gulick and L. Urwick. New York: Institute of Public Administration.

——. 1937b. "Science, Values and Administration." In *Papers on the Science of Administration*, edited by Luther Gulick and L. Urwick. New York: Institute of Public Administration.

——. 1948. *Administrative Reflections from World War II.* University, Ala.: University of Alabama Press.

Hart, David, and N. Dale Wright. 1998. "'The Civic Good': 'The Public Interest' of Civic Humanism." *Administrative Theory and Praxis* 20:406–421.

Hayek, Friedrich A. 1948. *Individualism and Economic Order.* Chicago: University of Chicago Press.

——. 1967. *Studies in Philosophy, Politics and Economics.* Chicago: University of Chicago Press.

——. 1973. *Law, Legislation and Liberty, Volume 1: Rules and Order.* Chicago: University of Chicago Press.

——. 1978. *New Studies in Philosophy, Politics, Economics and the History of Ideas.* Chicago: University of Chicago Press.

——. 1979. *The Counter-Revolution of Science: Studies on the Abuse of Reason.* Indianapolis: Liberty Press.

Hegel, G. W. F. 1952. *The Philosophy of Right.* Translated by T. M. Knox. New York: Oxford University Press.

——. 1956. *The Philosophy of History.* Translated by J. Sibree. New York: Dover Publications.

——. 1983. *Hegel's Lectures on the History of Philosophy, Volume 2.* Translated by E. S. Haldane and Frances H. Simson. New Jersey: Humanities Press.

Heller, Agnes, and Ferenc Fehér. 1988. *The Postmodern Political Condition.* New York: Columbia University Press.

Henderson, William O. 1965. *Studies in the Economic Policy of Frederick the Great.* New York: Augustus M. Kelley.

Himmelfarb, Gertrude. 1998. "Democratic Remedies for Social Disorders." *Public Interest* 131:3–24.

Holdsworth, William. 1967. *A History of English Law, Volume 6.* London: Methuen and Company and Sweet and Maxwell.

Hume, David. 1984. *A Treatise of Human Nature*. New York: Penguin Books.

———. 1987. *Essays: Moral, Political and Literary*. Indianapolis: Liberty Classics.

Hunter, James Davison. 1990. *Culture Wars: The Struggle to Define America*. New York: Basic Books.

———. 1994. *Before the Shooting Begins: Searching for Democracy in America's Culture War*. New York: Free Press.

Huntington, Samuel P. 1968. *Political Order in Changing Societies*. New Haven, Conn.: Yale University Press.

———. 1996. *The Clash of Civilizations and the Remaking of World Order*. New York: Simon and Schuster.

Iggers, Georg G. 1972. *The Doctrine of Saint-Simon: An Exposition*. New York: Schocken Books.

Johnson, Hubert C. 1975. *Frederick the Great and His Officials*. New Haven, Conn.: Yale University Press.

Karl, Barry Dean. 1963. *Executive Reorganization and Reform in the New Deal: The Genesis of Administrative Management, 1900–1939*. Cambridge: Harvard University Press.

Kelman, Steven. 1987. *Making Public Policy: A Hopeful View of American Government*. New York: Basic Books.

Knight, Frank H. 1982. *Freedom and Reform: Essays in Economics and Social Philosophy*. Indianapolis: Liberty Press.

Lambarde, William. 1972. *Eirenarcha*. London: Professional Books.

Lan, Zhiyong. 1997. "A Conflict Resolution Approach to Public Administration." *Public Administration Review* 57:27–35.

Lindblom, Charles E. 1959. "The Science of Muddling Through." *Public Administration Review* 29:79–88.

———. 1990. *Inquiry and Change: The Troubled Attempts to Understand and Shape Society*. New Haven, Conn.: Yale University Press.

Lindenfeld, David F. 1997. *The Practical Imagination: The German Sciences of State in the Nineteenth Century*. Chicago: University of Chicago Press.

List, Friedrich. 1904. *The National System of Political Economy*. Translated by Sampson S. Lloyd. London: Longmans, Green.

Locke, John. 1939. "An Essay Concerning the True Origin, Extent and End of Civil Government." In *The English Philosophers from Bacon to Mill*, edited by Edwin A. Burtt. New York: Modern Library.

Long, Norton. 1949. "Power and Administration." *Public Administration Review* 9:257–264.

Lyotard, Jean-François. 1984. *The Postmodern Condition: A Report on Knowledge.* Translated by Geoff Bennington and Brian Massumi. Minneapolis: University of Minnesota Press.

———. 1988. *The Differend: Phrases in Dispute.* Translated by Georges Van Den Abbeele. Minneapolis: University of Minnesota Press.

———. 1993. *The Postmodern Explained.* Minneapolis: University of Minnesota Press.

Lyotard, Jean-François, and Jean-Loup Thébaud. 1985. *Just Gaming.* Translated by Wlad Godzich. Minneapolis: University of Minnesota Press.

McCloskey, Donald N. 1990. *If You're So Smart: The Narrative of Economic Expertise.* Chicago: University of Chicago Press.

McSwite, O. C. 1997. *Legitimacy in Public Administration: A Discourse Analysis.* Thousand Oaks, Calif.: Sage Publications.

Mayo, Elton. 1946. *The Human Problems of an Industrial Civilization.* Boston: Harvard University.

Meier, Kenneth J. 1979. *Politics and the Bureaucracy: Policy-Making in the Fourth Branch of Government.* North Scituate, Mass.: Duxbury Press.

———. 1997. "Bureaucracy and Democracy: The Case for More Bureaucracy and Less Democracy." *Public Administration Review* 57:193–199.

Meinecke, Friedrich. 1962. *Machiavellism: The Doctrine of Raison d' État and Its Place in Modern History.* Translated by Douglas Scott. New Haven, Conn.: Yale University Press.

Mitchell, Terence R., and William G. Scott. 1987. "Leadership Failures, the Distrusting Public, and Prospects of the Administrative State." *Public Administration Review* 47:445–452.

———. 1988. "The Barnard-Simon Contribution: A Vanished Legacy." *Public Administration Quarterly* 12:348–368.

Moore, Barrington, Jr. 1966. *Social Origins of Dictatorship and Democracy: Lord and Peasant in the Making of the Modern World.* Boston: Beacon Press.

Morgan, Douglas. 1996. "Institutional Survival in the Postmodern Age: Administrative Practice and the American Constitutional Legacy." *Administrative Theory and Praxis* 18(2):42–56.

Mosher, Frederick C. 1968. *Democracy and the Public Service*. New York: Oxford University Press.

Nagel, Stuart S., and C. E. Teasley III. 1998. "Diverse Perspectives for Public Policy Analysis." In *Handbook of Public Administration*, 2d ed., edited by Jack Rabin, W. Bartley Hildreth, and Gerald J. Miller. New York: Marcel Dekker.

Nathan, Richard P. 1995. "Reinventing Government: What Does It Mean?" *Public Administration Review* 55:213–215.

Nef, John U. 1964. *Industry and Government in France and England, 1540–1640*. Ithaca, N.Y.: Cornell Paperbacks.

Notestein, Wallace. 1954. "The Justices of the Peace." In *The English People on the Eve of Colonization, 1603–1630*. New York: Harper and Row.

Oakeshott, Michael. 1975. *On Human Conduct*. Oxford: Clarendon Press.

———. 1991. *Rationalism in Politics and Other Essays*. Indianapolis: Liberty Press.

———. 1993. *Morality and Politics in Modern Europe: The Harvard Lectures*. New Haven, Conn.: Yale University Press.

———. 1996. *The Politics of Faith and the Politics of Scepticism*. New Haven, Conn.: Yale University Press.

Osborne, David, and Ted Gaebler. 1993. *Reinventing Government: How the Entrepreneurial Spirit Is Transforming the Public Sector*. New York: Penguin Books.

Osborne, David, and Peter Plastrik. 1997. *Banishing Bureaucracy: The Five Strategies for Reinventing Government*. New York: Addison Wesley.

Pangle, Thomas L. 1990. "The Philosophic Understandings of Human Nature Informing the Constitution." In *Confronting the Constitution: The Philosophical Challenge to Locke, Montesquieu, Jefferson, and the Federalists from Utilitarianism, Historicism, Marxism, Freudianism, Pragmatism, Existentialism . . .*, edited by Allan Bloom. Washington D.C.: AEI Press.

Parry, Geraint. 1963. "Enlightened Government and Its Critics in Eighteenth-Century Germany." *Historical Journal* 6:178–192.

Person, Harlow S. 1972. Foreword to *Scientific Management*, by Frederick Winslow Taylor. Westport, Conn.: Greenwood Press.

Poggi, Gianfranco. 1978. *The Development of the Modern State: A Sociological Introduction*. Stanford, Calif.: Stanford University Press.

Polanyi, Michael. 1941. "The Growth of Thought in Society." *Economica* 8:428–456.

———. 1998. *The Logic of Liberty.* Indianapolis: Liberty Fund.

Reich, Robert, ed. 1988. *The Power of Public Ideas.* Cambridge: Ballinger Publishing.

Robbins, Lionel. 1947. *The Economic Problem in Peace and War: Some Reflections on Objectives and Mechanisms.* London: Macmillan.

Rohr, John A. 1986. *To Run a Constitution: The Legitimacy of the Administrative State.* Lawrence, Kan.: University of Kansas Press.

Rorty, Richard. 1989. *Contingency, Irony, and Solidarity.* Cambridge: Cambridge University Press.

———. 1991a. *Essays on Heidegger and Others: Philosophical Papers, Volume 2.* Cambridge: Cambridge University Press.

———. 1991b. *Objectivity, Relativism, and Truth: Philosophical Papers, Volume 1.* Cambridge: Cambridge University Press.

Rosenberg, Hans. 1966. *Bureaucracy, Aristocracy, and Autocracy: The Prussian Experience, 1660–1815.* Cambridge, Mass.: Harvard University Press.

Rosenbloom, David H. 1993. "Have an Administrative Rx? Don't Forget the Politics." *Public Administration Review* 53:503–507.

———. 1999. "Administrative Reform in the New Millennium: Diagnosis, Prescription, and the Limits of Transferability." *Administrative Theory and Praxis* 21:491–496.

Rosenbloom, David H., and Rosemary O'Leary. 1997. *Public Administration and Law.* 2d. ed. New York: Marcel Dekker.

Saint-Simon, Henri De. 1964. *Social Organization, the Science of Man and Other Writings.* Translated by Felix Markham. New York: Harper Torchbooks.

Schlesinger, Arthur M. 1998. *The Disuniting of America: Reflections on a Multicultural Society.* Revised and enlarged edition. New York: W. W. Norton.

Schmoller, Gustav. 1989. *The Mercantile System and Its Historical Significance.* New York: Augustus M. Kelley.

Schultze, Charles L. 1968. *The Politics and Economics of Public Spending.* Washington D.C.: Brookings Institution.

Sharkansky, Ira. 1997. "What a Political Scientist Can Tell a Policymaker about the Likelihood of Success or Failure." In *Classics of Public Administration*, 4th ed., edited by Jay M. Shafritz and Albert C. Hyde. Fort Worth, Tex.: Harcourt Brace.

Simon, Herbert A. 1976. *Administrative Behavior: A Study of Decision-Making Processes in Administrative Organization.* 3d ed. New York: Macmillan.

Skocpol, Theda. 1985. "Bringing the State Back In: Strategies of Analysis in Current Research." In *Bringing the State Back In,* edited by Peter B. Evans, Dietrich Rueschemeyer, and Theda Skocpol. Cambridge: Cambridge University Press.

Skowronek, Stephen. 1982. *Building a New American State: The Expansion of National Administrative Capacities, 1877–1920.* Cambridge: Cambridge University Press.

Skyrme, Thomas. 1994. *History of the Justices of the Peace.* Chichester, England: Barry Rose and the Justice of the Peace.

Small, Albion W. 1909. *The Cameralists: The Pioneers of German Social Polity.* Chicago: University of Chicago.

Smith, James A. 1991. *The Idea Brokers: Think Tanks and the Rise of the New Policy Elite.* New York: Free Press.

Smith, Preserved. 1962. *The Enlightenment, 1687–1776.* New York: Collier Books.

Spicer, Michael W. 1995. *The Founders, the Constitution, and Public Administration: A Conflict in Worldviews.* Washington, D.C.: Georgetown University Press.

Stillman, Richard J. II. 1990. "The Peculiar 'Stateless' Origins of American Public Administration and Consequences for Government Today." *Public Administration Review* 50:156–167.

———. 1991. *Preface to Public Administration.* New York: St. Martin's Press.

———. 1995. "The Refounding Movement in American Public Administration: From Rabid Anti-Statism to 'Mere' Anti-Statism in the 1990's." *Administrative Theory and Praxis* 17:29–45.

———. 1997. "American vs. European Public Administration: Does Public Administration Make the Modern State, or Does the State Make Public Administration?" *Public Administration Review* 57:332–346.

———. 1998. *Creating the American State: The Moral Reformers and the Modern Administrative World They Made.* Tuscaloosa, Ala.: University of Alabama Press.

Stokey, Edith, and Richard Zeckhauser. 1978. *A Primer for Policy Analysis.* New York: W. W. Norton.

Strayer, Joseph R. 1970. *On the Medieval Origins of the Modern State.* Princeton, N.J.: Princeton University Press.

Taylor, Frederick Winslow. 1998. *The Principles of Scientific Management*. New York: Dover Publications.

Tocqueville, Alexis de. 1969. *Democracy in America*. Translated by George Lawrence. New York: Harper and Row.

Trevelyan, G. M. 1930. *England under the Stuarts*. New York: G. P. Putnam's Sons.

———. 1942a. *English Social History*. New York: David McKay.

———. 1942b. *A Shortened History of England*. New York: Longmans, Green.

Urwick, L. 1937. "Organization as a Technical Problem." In *Papers on the Science of Administration*, edited by Luther Gulick and L. Urwick. New York: Institute of Public Administration.

Waldo, Dwight. 1983. "The Perdurability of the Politics-Administration Dichotomy: Woodrow Wilson and the Identity Crisis in Public Administration." In *Politics and Administration: Woodrow Wilson and American Public Administration*, edited by Jack Rabin and James S. Bowman. New York: Marcel Dekker.

———. 1984. *The Administrative State*. New York: Holmes and Meier.

Wamsley, Gary L., Robert Bacher, Charles T. Goodsell, Phillip Kronenburg, John A. Rohr, Cammilla M. Stivers, Orion F. White, and James F. Wolf. 1990. *Refounding Public Administration*. Newbury Park, Calif.: Sage Publications.

Webb, Sydney, and Beatrice Webb. 1963. *English Local Government: The Parish and the County*. London: Frank Cass.

Weber, Max. 1946. *Essays in Sociology*. Translated by H. H. Gerth and C. Wright Mills. New York: Oxford University Press.

———. 1947. *The Theory of Social and Economic Organization*. Translated by A. M. Henderson and Talcott Parsons. New York: Free Press.

White, Leonard D. 1926. *Introduction to the Study of Public Administration*. New York: Macmillan.

Wildavsky, Aaron. 1979. *Speaking Truth to Power: The Art and Craft of Policy Analysis*. Boston: Little, Brown.

Willcox, William Bradford. 1940. *Gloucestershire: A Study in Local Government, 1590–1640*. New Haven, Conn.: Yale University Press.

Wills, Garry, ed. 1982. *The Federalist Papers by Alexander Hamilton, James Madison, and John Jay*. New York: Bantam Books.

Wilson, James Q. 1989. *Bureaucracy: What Government Agencies Do and Why They Do It*. New York: Basic Books.

Wilson, Woodrow. 1887. "The Study of Administration." *Political Science Quarterly* 2:197–222.

——. 1889. *The State: Elements of Historical and Practical Problems.* Boston: D. C. Heath.

——. 1956. *Congressional Government.* Cleveland: Meridian Books.

Wittgenstein, Ludwig. 1960. *The Blue and Brown Books: Preliminary Studies for the "Philosophical Investigations."* New York: Harper Torchbooks.

Wolin, Sheldon. 1960. *Politics and Vision: Continuity and Innovation in Western Political Thought.* Boston: Little, Brown.

Wright, N. Dale, and David Hart. 1996. "The 'Public Interest': What We Are Not Leaving Our Posterity." *Administrative Theory and Praxis* 18(2):14–28.

Zanetti, Lisa A., and Adrian N. Carr. 1998. "Exploring the Psychodynamics of Political Change." *Administrative Theory and Praxis* 20:358–376.

Index

abuse of power, 20, 76
Adams, Guy B., 64
Adams, Henry Baxter, 48
administration, apparatus of, 8, 26–28, 33, 34, 43, 46, 70, 76, 81, 83, 88, 112, 125, 128
Administrative Behavior (Simon), 59
administrative independence, 110, 113–124, 126
administrative juridicism, 110, 115–124, 126
administrative law, 120, 136
administrative technology, 27–30
African Americans, 101, 106–107
American Economic Association, 25–26
American Social Science Association, 25
anti-administration, 122
Atlantis (Bacon), 22
Atomic Energy Commission, 101

Bacon, Sir Francis, 7, 22–23, 54, 125; *Atlantis*, 22
Banta, Martha, 55
Barker, J. Ellis, 47
Barnard, Chester, 65
Barzelay, Michael, 62
Behn, Robert D., 62, 63–64
Beloff, Max, 43
Bentham, Jeremy, 29
Berlin, Isaiah, 11–12, 16, 19, 24, 91–92, 97–98, 102, 104, 105, 130–133
Blacksburg School, 137
Bluntschli, Johann K., 44–45, 48
Brownlow, Louis, 56
Brownlow Committee, 56
Buchanan, James M., 106

Burke, Edmund, 74–75, 129, 138
business, as a model for public administration, 6, 7, 49–50, 53, 59–60, 63

Calvinist states, 16
cameralists, 8, 34–35, 38–39, 42–43, 47, 48, 69. *See also* Prussia, government and administration of
Carey, Henry C., 46
Carr, Adrian N., 67–68
Carroll, James D., 7
Catron, Bayard L., 67
Charles I of England, 113, 118
chief executive, 43, 51, 56, 63–64, 70, 82, 120–121
civil association: vision of the state as, ix, 21–22, 71–75; historical practice of, 75–77, 109–111; and the Constitution, 77–80; and public administration, 80–83, 86–87, 108, 109–111, 126, 129, 134–139; and social science, 83–88; and the postmodern condition, 102–108, 130
Civil War, American, 25, 128
Civil War, English, 76–77, 113
Cohen, Steven, 62
Coke, Sir Edward, 120
common law, 76, 115, 116–117
comparative public administration, 132–133
conflict resolution, field of, 136
Constitution, the: and civil association, 77–80; and public administration, 80–83, 100–101, 127–130, 137; and postmodernism, 105. *See also*

constitutionalism
constitutionalism, 20, 105–107, 129–130, 137–138, 139. *See also* Constitution, the
Countrey Justice, The (Dalton), 116
courts and public administration, 101, 120, 136
critical theorists, 66–68
Croly, Herbert, 46–47
culture wars, 92–95

Dahl, Richard A., 127, 130
Dalton, Michael, *Countrey Justice, The*, 116
Davies, Margaret Gay, 113
democracy, 10, 21, 48, 52, 56, 57, 59, 69, 120
Denhardt, Robert D., 67
Dennison, Henry, 55
depression, economic, 71, 82, 99
differend, the, 97
DiIulio, John J., Jr., 62
Dorn, Walter L., 34, 35–37, 40–42
Douglas, Roger, 100
Dyson, Kenneth, H. F., 13

Edward III of England, 111
Eirenarcha (Lambarde), 116
Eisenhower, General Dwight, 6
Elizabeth I of England, 111
Ely, Richard, 25–26, 45
enlightenment, 16, 31, 33, 46, 90
Evans, Peter B., 10

Farmer, David J., 122, 132
Federalist Papers, 77, 106. *See also* Hamilton, Alexander; Madison, James
Fehér, Ferenc, 90
Finer, Herman, 122
Fletcher, Anthony, 113–115, 118
Follett, Mary Parker, 57–58
Foucault, Michel, 19–20, 28–31, 96
founders, the, 79, 80, 83, 137, 138. *See also* Hamilton, Alexander; Madison, James
Fox, Charles J., 129–130

France, 33–34, 43, 47–49, 74, 111
Frederickson, H. George, 66
Frederick the Great: writings of, 34, 37–38, 42; as ruler and administrator (*see* Prussia, government and administration of)
Frederick William I of Prussia, 33, 34, 47
French Revolution, 16, 74
Fukuyama, Francis, 129

Gaebler, Ted, 3, 5, 7, 99
Geneva, 16
Germany, 33, 34, 36, 43–49, 111
Gleason, J. H., 118
Glorious Revolution, 77
Gooch, G. P., 42, 43–44
Gore, Al, 5–6, 7
Gray, John, 90, 94–95, 103–104, 109
Gulick, Luther, 8, 53, 55, 56, 98

Habermas, Jürgen, 67
Hamilton, Alexander, 79
Harmon, Michael M., 67
Hart, David, 137–138
Hayek, Friedrich A., 15, 84–85, 86
Hegel, G. W. F., 44, 48, 57
Heller, Agnes, 90
Henderson, W. O., 36
Himmelfarb, Gertrude, 93–94
historical school of economics, 45, 48
history, use of in public administration enquiry, 132, 133, 139
Holdsworth, William, 115, 117, 118
human relations school of public administration, 58, 68
Hume, David, 74, 138
Hunter, James Davison, 92–94
Huntington, Samuel P., 109–110, 129

incommensurabilities, 90–93, 95, 98, 104
individuality, emergence of, 75–76
instrumental rationalism, 64, 68, 98, 134

James I of England, 112, 118
Johns Hopkins University, 48

Justi, Johann Heinrich Gottlob von, 34–35, 38–39, 42–43, 47
justices of the peace of Stuart England: and civil association, 109–111; responsibilities of, 111–113; independence of, 113–115, 117–118; and law, 115–117, 118; and American public administration, 119–121, 123–124

Karl, Barry Dean, 48
Kelman, Steven, 120
Kennedy, President John F., 6
Knight, Frank H., 87

Lambarde, William: *Eirenarcha*, 116
Lan, Zhiyong, 136
language games, 91, 92, 95–97, 100, 102–105, 107, 121–123
law and American public administration, 119–121, 136
legislature, 10, 63–64, 78–79, 80, 101
liberty, 18, 44, 52, 73–74, 77–79, 96, 98, 104, 133–134
Lindblom, Charles E., 69, 87, 127
Lindenfeld, David F., 35
List, Friedrich, 44
Locke, John, 73–74, 78, 80, 106, 109, 138; *Second Treatise of Government*, 73, 77
Long, Norton, 81–82
Louis XIV of France, 33–34
Lyotard, Jean-François, 89, 91, 97, 102, 104

McSwite, O. C., 64
Madison, James, 77–79, 130
Mayo, Elton, 58–59
Meier, Kenneth J., 65
Meinecke, Friedrich, 45–46
mercantilism, 30, 35, 111
Merriam, Charles E., 56
metanarratives, 89–90, 95, 102, 106, 130
Miller, Hugh T., 129–130
Mitchell, Terence R., 65, 86–87
monism, 19, 91–92, 97–98, 102
Morgan, Douglas, 138

Mosher, Frederick C., 48

Nagel, Stuart S., 61
Nathan, Richard P., 7
National Performance Review, 5–7
Native Americans, 106–107, 122–123
Nef, John U., 117, 118
neo-Marxism, 67, 130
new public administration, 66, 68

Oakeshott, Michael, 8, 13–21, 26–28, 31, 43, 71–73, 75–77, 80, 103, 106, 133–136
O'Leary, Rosemary, 101, 120, 136
Osborne, David, 3, 5, 7, 99–100

Pangle, Thomas L., 73
panopticon, 29
Parliament, English, 75, 76–77, 109–110, 113, 118
Parry, Geraint, 39
Person, Harlow S., 54
phenomenology, 67
Plastrik, Peter, 99–100
pluralism, 7, 82, 90, 91, 95, 99–100, 102, 104
pluralist writers, 69, 101, 127, 130
Poggi, Gianfranco, 34
Polanyi, Michael, 15, 25, 84
policy analysis, 8–9, 51, 59, 61–62, 68
political theory in public administration enquiry, 1–4, 9, 10–12, 64, 68–69, 131–132, 139
population, 19–20, 30–31, 38–39
positivism, 3, 23, 125–126
postmodern condition, the, ix, 89–92, 126; cultural conflict in, 92–95; and purposive association, 95–98; and public administration, 98–102, 121–123, 129–130; and civil association, 102–105, 106–108, 130; and constitutionalism, 105–108, 130
Privy Council, 112, 114, 116–117
Prussia, government and administration of, 8, 33–37, 40–42; influence on

political thought, 8, 43–47, 50, 125; and American public administration, 8, 48–50. *See also* cameralists; Frederick the Great

public administration, modern mainstream writings in, 8–9, 51, 59–66, 68; critics of, 51, 65–68

public administration orthodoxy, 8–9, 51–56, 139; dissenters from, 56–59, 62

public management writers, 51, 62, 63–64, 65, 68, 99, 121, 125–126

purposive association: vision of the state as, 7, 14–16, 21–22; and Prussia, 8, 33, 35, 38, 39, 43, 47, 50, 125; and public administration writers, 8, 51–53, 56–57, 59, 63–66, 68, 69, 125–126; ends of, 16–18; government of, 18–21; advocates of, 22–23; and science, 23–26, 87; and administrative power, 26–28, 30, 31; and the Constitution, 78, 80–83; and postmodernism, 95–98, 107, 126. *See also* teleocratic government, vision of

purposive state. *See* purposive association; teleocratic government, vision of

quarter sessions, 112–113, 118

rationalist worldview, 24

Reich, Robert, 65

reinventing government, 3–7, 63, 68, 99–100, 121, 124–126, 132–133

return to the state movement, 10, 13, 128

Richelieu, Cardinal de, 33–34

Robbins, Lionel, 17

Rohr, John A., 119, 137

Roosevelt, President Franklin D., 56, 82–83

Rorty, Richard, 102, 105–106, 122–123

Rosenberg, Hans, 37, 41

Rosenbloom, David H., 3, 101, 120, 136

Rousseau, Jean-Jacques, 82

Rueschemeyer, Dietrich, 10

Saint-Simon, Henri De, 23, 24

Schlesinger, Arthur M., 94

Schmoller, Gustav, 45, 48

Schultze, Charles L., 61

science, 22, 23, 89, 90, 106, 130; in public administration, 2–3, 10–12, 38, 48–49, 53–55, 58–62, 66, 68, 69, 131–132, 139; and purposive association, 23–26, 87; limits of within a civil association, 83–88

scientific management, 54–55

Scott, William G., 65, 86–87

Second Treatise of Government (Locke), 73, 77

separation of powers, 20, 79, 83, 119, 127

Sharkansky, Ira, 61

Simon, Herbert A., 3, 8–9, 51, 59–60, 64–65, 98–99, 125; *Administrative Behavior*, 59

Skocpol, Theda, 10, 13

Skowronek, Stephen, 128

Skyrme, Sir Thomas, 118

Small, Albion W., 35, 38, 47, 48

Smith, James A., 25

Smith, Preserved, 47

Soviet Union, collapse of, 90

state, the: neglect of, 1–4; definition of, 13–14. *See also* civil association; purposive association

Stillman, Richard J., II, 1, 2, 13, 50, 80, 128–129

Stokey, Edith, 61

Taylor, Frederick Winslow, 8, 54–55

Teasley, C. E., 61

teleocratic government, vision of, 18–21, 31, 70, 71, 87, 88, 125, 129; in reinventing government, 5–7, 63; and Prussia, 33, 35, 38, 39, 43, 47; in public administration, 51–53, 56, 59–66, 68, 98–102, 120, 135; constitutional constraints on, 80–83, 126; and postmodern condition, 89, 95–102, 107, 126. *See also* purposive association

terror, 97

therapeutic state, 16, 59, 67–68

Tocqueville, Alexis De, 119

Trevelyan, G. M., 111, 118

University of Chicago, 48

Urwick, L., 1

U.S. Public Health Service, 101

values, role of in the study of public administration, 3, 11, 64, 68, 130–134

Waldo, Dwight, 2, 3, 8, 52, 53, 55, 69, 131, 139

war and purposive association, 17, 71

Ward, Frank, 86

Webb, Beatrice, 116

Webb, Sydney, 116

Weber, Max, 45

White, Leonard D., 49, 52, 55, 98, 111, 112

Wildavsky, Aaron, 69

Willcox, William Bradford, 112, 117

Wilson, James Q., 83, 119, 120

Wilson, Woodrow, 3, 8, 48–49, 52, 53–54, 110–111, 127

Wolin, Sheldon, 60

World War I, 47, 49

World War II, 6, 17, 53, 71, 128

Wright, N. Dale, 137–138

Zanetti, Lisa A., 67–68

Zeckhauser, Richard, 61

Printed in the United States
29304LVS00007B/211-288